MW00416355

Simply ... this is a story that needs to be heard. One of courage, one of loyalty, one of leadership, and most importantly one of faith. Ricky Dickson's four-decade-plus professional journey to the CEO chair of one of America's most beloved brands in itself would be noteworthy but to ascend into leadership just as the company faced its most critical moment, that is a story only explained through a lens of faith and shared by Ricky in a profound way in *One Scoop at a Time*!

—DOUG MCNAMEE
President of Field & Stream, Former President of Magnolia

One Scoop at a Time is a marvelous title for a book that tells the story of the tremendous growth of one of America's most beloved ice cream companies. And, it is the story of a man who became a great success himself along with the remarkable success of the Blue Bell brand. Ricky Dickson used his gift of communication in writing *One Scoop at a Time* to capture one's attention and "keep it." His writing style is conversational. His stories are easily relatable. His recorded remembrances of his journey from boyhood to successful executive are compelling and easily relatable to every reader. I found *One Scoop at a Time* easy to read and hard to put down. I would recommend you get a big bowl of BLUE BELL'S COOKIES 'N CREAM, a comfortable chair, and treat yourself to the exciting story recorded here.

—NICK GARLAND
Retired Senior Pastor - First Baptist Broken Arrow Oklahoma

Prepare to be inspired and empowered! Ricky's book is a compelling blend of authenticity, leadership principles, and heartfelt wisdom. With refreshing honesty, he tackles life's challenges head-on, guiding readers toward a path of joy and purpose. Whether you're a leader, an entrepreneur pursuing a dream, a Christian seeking to make a difference in the workplace, a parent navigating the journey of parenthood, or simply someone seeking guidance in everyday life, this book is for you. Thank you, Ricky, for your transparency and for sharing a book that adds value to the lives of all who read it!

—BRIAN MILLS
Pastor at Together We Church

"I had the privilege to work with Ricky for over twenty-five years. His ability to tell a story is only surpassed by his love for Christ. He is a walking example of how a Christian should conduct themselves and I am happy that this book will allow others to enjoy his stories, and the lessons that accompany them, as we all continue learning how to build faith from our fears."

—JIMMY LAWHORN
President, Blue Bell Creameries

How can you be CEO of a multimillion-dollar company, oversee hundreds of co-workers in multiple states, survive storms corporately & personally—and still love God, trust His Word, & honor His Son? Ricky Dickson's story will amaze you, challenge you, & dare you to believe for more. He is a Joseph, a Daniel in our day—a lover of God placed in a completely secular environment. And he's been my friend for almost forty years.

—DR. DAVID WALKER
Senior Pastor, Alamo City Church

Ricky Dickson has written a book so full of goodness that, if you could turn it into a new Blue Bell flavor, it would become an instant bestseller. I had the privilege of serving as Ricky's pastor for several years as he led Blue Bell. The powerful and poignant stories he shares in this book reflect the man I know—full of joy and humility. Just like a half gallon of Blue Bell should be enjoyed one scoop at a time, this book should be enjoyed one chapter at a time as you reflect on how God has designed you to live for Jesus. Taste this book and see that the Lord is good!

—PHILLIP BETHANCOURT
Lead Pastor, Central Church, College Station, TX

I worked with Ricky Dickson for years, and I've seen his leadership and integrity in action. He has a wealth of knowledge and experience to share that would be useful in the ice cream industry or life in general.

—DOUG MARTIN
Blue Bell General Counsel and Vice President of Compliance

Ricky Dickson offers us all an inspiring and encouraging story that I have found hard to put down. *One Scoop at a Time* is marked with deep faith and practical instruction that will help all readers navigate their good days ... and their hard days. This is welcome wisdom from a top-level CEO. I cannot recommend this book highly enough. Pick it up and start reading!

—DR. HEATH A. THOMAS
President, Oklahoma Baptist University
Associate Fellow, Kirby Laing Centre for Public Theology in Cambridge, UK

Stories & Lessons from Fear to Faith

One Scoop at a Time

Ricky Dickson

Former CEO & President of Blue Bell Creameries

Unless otherwise indicated, all Scripture quotations are taken from NLT.
Scripture quotations are taken from the Holy Bible, New Living Translation, copyright ©1996, 2004, 2015 by Tyndale House Foundation. Used by permission of Tyndale House Publishers, Carol Stream, Illinois 60188. All rights reserved.

Fedd Books
P.O. Box 341973
Austin, TX 78734

www.thefeddagency.com

Published in association with The Fedd Agency, Inc., a literary agency.

ISBN: 978-1-957616-70-4

LCCN: 2024935561

Printed in the United States of America

To my beautiful wife, Anita.
My biggest cheerleader, supporter, and best friend.
Thank you for believing in me.
I love you.

Table of Contents

Foreword

Few things bring us to our knees like fear.

Fear is a powerful emotion, whether it's fear of failure or the future. How we manage that emotion will make us or break us. You can draw closer to God, or you can distance yourself.

When life is good, walking with God is relatively easy. It's when things get complicated—when fear wiggles its way into our minds and hearts—that we find ourselves at God's feet.

How do we face those fears?

How do we find the courage to trust God?

How do we experience the peace that passes understanding?

I had the pleasure of meeting Ricky Dickson, CEO and President of Blue Bell Creameries, several years ago. Actually, I met the ice cream first. And as a connoisseur of ice cream, can I take a moment to praise God? So good.

Ricky is an incredibly gifted leader, but he's also down-to-earth. I like that combination because that's what I see in Jesus. He didn't just do miracles, Jesus also washed feet. Ricky is that kind of leader. Like all of us, Ricky has faced his fair share of fear. Of course, when you lead hundreds of employees and have millions of customers, the stakes are a little higher! This book is full of leadership lessons that are incredibly practical and relatable. It's also an inside look at how Ricky's relationship with God has helped him navigate the twists and turns of leadership.

Ricky is both kind-hearted and light-hearted. A sense of humor is one of those underestimated qualities of great leaders. You'll find yourself smiling as you read *One Scoop at a Time*. It's an open invitation to step into your destiny. How? By moving from fear to faith. And that starts with surrendering your life and leadership to God.

In a fast-moving and rapidly changing world, it's easy to get stuck in the cycle of fear being pushed our way every day. It's easy to let what you cannot do keep you from doing what you can. It's easy to believe that you don't make a difference. Ricky's life is evidence that everything we do—big or small—matters more than we think! Stop letting fear dictate your decisions and start letting faith call the shots.

Can I make one recommendation as you read? Pick a flavor, any favor, but why not eat a pint of Blue Bell Ice Cream while you read? I believe you'll be a better leader at the end of this book. How will it happen? One scoop, one step, one day at a time!

—MARK BATTERSON
New York Times Bestselling Author

Introduction

It was tradition as far back as anyone could remember for our board of directors to host a shareholder meeting every year in February. It was also tradition that once the officers of the company concluded their reports on the previous year's success, followed by new projections of optimism, the board would adjourn to a private room to elect the new slate of officers for the coming year. For almost one hundred years, this tradition included placing a member of the Kruse family at the head of the company, starting with E.F. Kruse from 1919 to 1951. Ed Kruse (E.F.'s son) from 1951 to 1993. Howard Kruse (Ed's brother) from 1993 to 2004 and then Paul Kruse (Ed's son) from 2004 to 2017.

On February 16, 2017, that tradition came to an end. With the announcement of Paul Kruse's retirement, the board of directors unanimously voted me as the new president of Blue Bell Creameries. Believe me, it was the shock of my life, and the nomination literally took my breath away. You could have driven a Mack Truck through the room and I don't think I would have noticed it. Reflecting on that day and the many years prior, it had become apparent that God was working in my life for such a time as this! Every step along the journey prepared me for the next position, and all I had to do is trust Him, *One Scoop at a Time.*

One Scoop at a Time is a collection of stories and fun experiences from my journey—from my college days to working for Blue Bell to personal events. All these moments left a profound effect on who I am today.

As a Christian, I have found that seeking God's will for my life has taken me on a journey through incredible highs and some deep lows. Trusting God's voice during those times can be difficult, but for most of my life I have found that during the struggles I have camped out the most at His feet.

Faith seems easy—until it gets hard. So, how can you find peace during the most difficult times of your life? How do you anchor a ship when the waves are tossing you about?

Recognizing God's voice is critical when trying to follow the path He has laid out for you. This is especially true when His directions don't make sense and become difficult, but it's in the struggle that He will strengthen you and provide an indescribable peace that can only come from Him.

Who or where you place your trust can also reveal where your faith truly lies. But when you eventually run out of options that the world has to offer, you are greeted with open arms by a Savior who loves you more than you can ever imagine. He isn't there to numb your pain; He's there to heal your heart. But you first must give it to Him.

God was always working behind the scenes to close doors I thought were best for me and open doors of opportunity I would have never anticipated.

It's hard to remember that God has a plan for you when you're consumed with worry and fear. Fear can manipulate your emotions in a heartbeat, drive you to your knees, or even warp your perception of reality. Fear can keep you up at night, and if it takes root, it can leave you empty and exasperated. If we aren't prepared to face fear with the tools the Lord has given us, we may wind up spiraling down a dark path.

Think back to some of your first childhood fears—the monster in the closet or even fear of trying something new at dinner like liver and onions. Those moments probably felt as visceral as the threat of heights or wasps or scorpions.

As we let go of our childhood fears, we take on new ones as adults like the fear of failure, the future, or even death. But how do we transition from fear to faith? How can we find the peace that passes all understanding? To journey through some of life's most turbulent seasons requires a strong rock to anchor to. My rock is my faith in Jesus Christ. In the toughest situations, I can rest in His love and ask for direction. It's my faith in Christ that has sustained me through each of the most difficult challenges.

Even though my life has been filled with many blessings, there have also been extremely difficult times that challenged my faith, leaving me searching for answers.

From learning that my four-month-old son had been diagnosed with viral meningitis to a failed marriage to learning that a pathogen had been discovered in our ice cream at work, each conflict drove me to my knees and required a deep faith in Christ to give me strength to make it through.

I've learned that the antidote to fear is faith, and transforming fear into faith requires first dying to oneself. Finding peace in the middle of a trial requires you to look up instead of looking in, and it can be an amazing road to travel, once you have released your fear to God. One of my all-time favorite verses in the Bible is found in Philippians 4:6–7:

⁶ Do not be anxious about anything, but in every situation, by prayer and petition, with thanksgiving, present your requests to God. ⁷ And the peace of God, which transcends all understanding, will guard your hearts and your minds in Christ Jesus.

It's my anchor verse, and even in the worst of situations, I come running back to its promise.

I once heard a story of a small West Texas town that was experiencing a major summer drought. Temperatures soared to over 100 degrees every afternoon, and the land had become desolate and dry. Farmers had grown concerned that without any rain, the land would eventually swallow up their herds of cattle. As with any disaster, time was of the essence, and all the town could do was pray.

Led by the town's pastor, word spread that there would be a city-wide prayer meeting the upcoming Sunday morning. Everyone was encouraged to come expecting a miracle. On Sunday, the church was filled beyond capacity with the overflow crowd stretching out into the parking lot. After a few songs of praise, the pastor began to offer up a prayer for rain, reminding God how desperate times had become. One after another, people from all over continued this intercessory of desperation, holding out hope that God would answer.

Way off in the distance, a small white cloud began to form. It was hard to see with the naked eye, but it was indeed a cloud. As they continued to pray, the cloud began to expand, and other clouds began to emerge. Then the congregation heard the sound of distant thunder. Could it be? Could God be behind this—to show his power and faithfulness to this small Texas town?

"Keep praying," the pastor told the congregation, as hundreds joined in intercession, expecting a miracle.

Then the clouds grew, and a breeze began to blow throughout the city. Finally, the winds became stronger, the clouds came together, and lighting and thunder came to center stage.

"Keep praying!" yelled the pastor from the pulpit. As the entire crowd lifted up their voice in prayer, the first drops of rain began to fall on the land below. The rain became stronger, and the people ran out into the streets, celebrating the wonder and goodness that the Lord provided. People, young and old, were jumping up and down while others hugged each other for this wonderful miracle.

In the middle of the celebration, the crowds suddenly stopped in their tracks, and everyone looked toward the middle of the street. With rain pouring down, there stood a young girl with an umbrella open above her head. The whole town had all come to pray for rain, but only this young woman came prepared for the miracle.

Even though God doesn't always work as fast as I would like, I have learned to trust His timing as much as His answer. The key is to be ready when He moves—and trust me, He's always moving … all to bring Him glory.

So, I pray that this book will give you a little insight into Blue Bell Creameries, and relive some of the memories that have shaped our company as well as my own life, but most importantly, I pray it strengthens your faith in ways that only God can do.

01

The History

It doesn't feel like summer without ice cream, so it's not surprising that Blue Bell's origin story begins in the heart of South-Central Texas, in the town of Brenham.

To understand the mystique of Blue Bell ice cream, you must first understand the company's culture. The magic starts with our employees and their daily commitment to producing and delivering the best ice cream in markets all across the country. Many of our employees have called Blue Bell home for multiple generations, with over 25 percent serving for over twenty years. Along with making great-tasting ice cream, it's not uncommon for many to also help with farm or ranch duties at home, including working with cattle to grow and harvest crops.

The goal of "consistently meeting the expectation that drives the passion," as we like to say, is at the forefront of everything we do. In fact, making ice cream is all we do, so we have to get it right every day. It's something we've learned by tradition—having been in the ice cream business for over one hundred years.

But Blue Bell was once not synonymous with ice cream. Our founders started in the butter business.

It all began on a hot summer day back in August 1907. "The Brenham Creamery Company," as it was originally named, opened its doors selling butter. Using cream from farmers in the surrounding area, sour cream butter was churned daily and then made available for the local community. It wasn't until 1911 that the first hand-cranked concoctions of ice cream were created.

Using a metal can filled with ice and salt, employees captured the sweet combination of cream and a variety of sumptuous ice cream flavors.

Back then, we were only able to produce two gallons of ice cream a day. Those two gallons were sold immediately to the lucky locals ready to consume the delicious treat before it melted.

In 1936, the name was changed to Blue Bell Creameries, after the native wildflowers that grew in the area. In 1958, the company made the difficult decision to discontinue making butter and concentrate solely on making ice cream and related products. From 1960 until 1977, Blue Bell Supreme Ice Cream could only be found in Brenham, Austin, Houston, and the surrounding areas. By 1978, the company stretched to enter the Dallas-Fort Worth area and has continued to grow ever since.

FIRST ENCOUNTERS

In the late 1970s, I was introduced to Blue Bell in a unique way.

For our family, ice cream was one of a variety of dessert options that we had to choose from. We seemed to gravitate more to the cake and pie category, with vanilla ice cream used more as a topping.

While growing up in San Antonio (where Blue Bell wasn't yet available), we resorted to store-brand ice cream. But on rare occasions, Mom would pull out the ice cream maker and work her magic. She would combine her special ingredients into the metal container, insert the dasher, and we took turns with the cranking process. With ice, rock salt, and this rotating hand-cranked labor, we patiently work toward the enjoyment of the final product. Fresh strawberries or bananas were always a must, and licking the dasher heightened the entire experience.

While attending O.W. Holmes High School, I began dating the woman I thought would eventually become Mrs. Dickson. (Spoiler alert: She did not.)

With no specific direction, career path, or desire to attend a particular college, I knew one thing—I had a passion for her. And she had a passion for going to Baylor University in Waco, Texas. The choice was easy, *or so I thought.* Since she was a year behind me in school, I decided to attend McMurry College in Abilene, Texas my freshman year. This gave me the opportunity run track one more year before transferring to Baylor. That's a story for another book (a really small book at that).

In fall of 1978, our initial plan fell into place, and we found ourselves together again in Waco. As exciting as that seemed in theory, it became evident that God's path for our lives was different than what we had planned. After dating for over three years, we were long past the infatuation stage of our relationship and began to realize there were too many differences in our fundamental beliefs to make our relationship last.

Basically, instead of a path of Homemade Vanilla, our relationship had fallen on a Rocky Road. Recognizing this, we made the decision to go our separate ways. As difficult as this was, it was the right decision. One that we both had prayed over for clarity and one that He answered.

Now, after only a few days at Baylor, I found myself single again, with no major yet declared, and living off-campus, wondering why I

4 | *One Scoop at a Time*

had I even transferred in the first place. I desired more than anything to follow where God was leading, yet things seemed totally out of focus and now, almost out of control. Love can do that to you.

I eventually learned that I was exactly where God wanted me to be in order to prepare me for His future plans that I had prayed for.

When the struggle becomes so real, it's hard to see the hand of God working. Yet it was also a great place to begin the journey in trust. It's one thing to say you trust Christ, yet it's another to go follow the Lord's voice when it doesn't seem to make sense. I have learned that when I truly begin to walk by faith, the steps become easier to take.

Remember feeling terrified and excited when you were tossed in the air as a child by someone you trusted? Once you are back in their arms, the world is right again. As a father, there's nothing more exciting than to watch his child take those first initial steps with open arms, ready to catch them if they fall. Trusting comes when you know that He's there and will catch you. God waits with open arms.

> **"Trusting comes when you know that He's there and will catch you. God waits with open arms."**

Now in hindsight, I can see how God was moving in my life at this time, but it wasn't until a few years later that this all made sense. It was that relationship that got me to Baylor, fulfilling God's will for that season in my life. That's also what happens when our desires take over and we get out in front of God's voice. We can feel lost and fearful. Fortunately, God is extremely patient and has a way to bring us back in if we let Him.

In the fall of 1979, I finally landed on a major. Even though I still didn't have a clue about what I wanted to do after graduation, I zeroed in on a business degree, majoring in marketing with a minor in business journalism. It was a major that also only required nine hours of accounting. I began working for the Baylor campus newspaper *The Lariat,* as well as working as a runner at a local advertising agency. Both experiences gave me the opportunity to not only write, but also learn the creative side of advertising. Finding both areas fascinating, I began to consider working for a public relations or advertising company post-graduation. Fortunately, I left the door open for other options, but most importantly, I began to truly pray specifically for God's direction.

The foundation of my prayer life began at home and at an early age. I was so blessed to grow up with parents who stressed the importance of not just believing in Jesus but developing a relationship with Him. They taught me that in order to recognize His voice, you have to pour yourself over the scriptures and pray.

My father began many days early in the morning in his home office praying for the day. He was always ready to discuss a particular passage in scripture he had found intriguing. If you wanted guidance in a certain situation or dealing with a tough circumstance, you called Dad. His availability and openness were a great template for how we should approach our Heavenly Father.

Mom, on the other hand, was our prayer warrior. Throughout my life, she would always ask me how she could pray for me. Just knowing that kind of love and devotion gave me confidence, no matter the circumstance. Their examples of living a Christ-like life helped build the foundation for my prayer life, teaching me to always pray and seek God's perfect will for my life.

THE ASSIGNMENT

As exciting as the advertising and public relations world seemed, God's plan began to unfold in my junior year with a Consumer Relations class. Our assignment was simple: Choose any company you want and follow them throughout the semester. Then write a term paper explaining how they go about relating their product(s) and image to the public. This twenty-five-page, single-spaced — *on a typewriter* — paper seemed exciting, yet challenging, and I didn't know where it would take me.

So, I went back to my apartment, picked up the phone, and called my dad for advice. Dad was a great "go-to" when confronted with a challenge, and with a paper representing 75 percent of my grade, I needed a great "go-to."

Fortunately, Dad was at home, and after a quick update on current affairs at Baylor and an update on the family at home, I dove into my situation.

Calling home was also special and expensive, with each minute being billed to my land line account. I don't remember if it was a rotary dial or touch-tone phone, but cell phones, free long-distance, and texting were things we only dreamed about.

After explaining my dilemma with this unique request, Dad kind of laughed and said he might just have the perfect "sweet" solution. It just so happened that at the time, my dad was reading an article on this "little ice cream company" in Brenham, Texas, and thought it might be fun to select them for the project. Who doesn't like ice cream?

As a third generation dentist, any recommendation concerning sweets would normally be discouraged, but I could tell through his enthusiastic spirit that he was onto something. So I asked him to start the article over again, this time reading it aloud to me.

I decided I needed to try Blue Bell. At the time, Blue Bell wasn't available in Waco, so I planned a road trip and anticipated the taste of sweet ice cream. All for the sake of the project, of course.

After talking with Dad, I gathered what information I could from the article and, within two weeks, found myself at the main office at Blue Bell. On my initial call I was immediately connected with John Barnhill, Blue Bell's executive vice president and general sales manager. Being connected with the executive vice president was the last thing I expected, but his warm response matched the image I had from the article. After explaining the nature of the call, he agreed to an interview, and we set a time to meet.

Upon arrival, John welcomed me into his office and seemed to be as inquisitive about my project as I was of the company. My first impression was that he hadn't received very many requests like mine and enjoyed sharing details about the Blue Bell mystique. For approximately an hour and a half, John navigated through Blue Bell's rich history, stressing the importance of consistently making the best ice cream "in the country." The double meaning "in the country" was the image that seemed to be the common thread through all their advertising. The way he described the plant operation also seemed as if those that made the delicious flavors made each one as if they were making it for their families at home, and then they would sell whatever was left.

During the interview, Ed Kruse, the president and CEO, came in and joined the conversation. After introducing himself, he pivoted into question mode and, like John, he made me feel like I was part of the team instead of a student in college.

With Mr. Barnhill, a Longhorn, and Mr. Kruse, an Aggie, I'm not sure if they had ever visited with a student from Baylor before. The atmosphere was extremely welcoming, and their proud but humble approach to business made you want to be a part of the excitement they projected. If they could be so enthusiastic, I could only imagine others feeling the same throughout the company.

John stressed the importance of providing the best quality product at a value, which seemed to be at the center of everything they strived to do. It was more than just making ice cream though; it was creating memories. I soon realized this was the perfect company to have chosen to do my study on consumer behavior patterns, and my research needed to begin immediately.

As educational and rewarding as I found my visit to be, the only downfall was that we didn't get to enjoy any ice cream during our time together. So after returning to Waco, I asked a friend to join me on my quest and declared a road trip in search of Blue Bell. The closest city that carried Blue Bell products was in Temple, Texas, thirty miles south of town, so off we went.

Once in Temple, we located a grocery store right off the highway and went after this treasured iconic brand. Overcoming all the obstacles so far on my journey, I soon found the hardest decision to make of all: What flavors should I choose? Homemade Vanilla was supposed to be the closest to homemade ice cream, yet we both wanted something with a little more to it. After much deliberation and debate, we settled on Strawberries 'n Cream. We made our way to the checkout stand, grabbing a package of spoons on the way, then ran back to the car to start our journey home.

Nestled in the two front seats with spoons in hand, we dove into the experience of a lifetime. Just for the record, we were able to finish off the half gallon before crossing the city limits in Waco. Probably not a record, but we were pleased with our accomplishment. Talk about creating memories. I can still remember my first bite as if it were today.

The flavor exploded off the tip of my tongue, and each bite's freshness took me back to Mom's hand-cranked masterpieces. All the flavor without all the cranking. I can't imagine how many bowls of Blue Bell I have had since, nor am I going to try and count.

Throughout the semester, I became intrigued by what I discovered about Blue Bell. There was something unique and different about this company. The atmosphere and culture seemed to be as much about people as it was about making a profit. Open door policies, a first name basis between all employees, and a true family atmosphere that seemed incredibly inviting.

Don't get me wrong, all companies are there ultimately for making a profit, but it wasn't the only factor when defining success at Blue Bell. This philosophy requires great patience and determination, but also keeps you from growing too rapidly, compromising the foundation that has been established. Again, it really comes down to making the very best ice cream possible at a true value, while taking care of each employee and shareholder. This vision was clear, and everyone worked to achieve the goals set forth. By the end of the semester, I had accomplished the objective of writing the paper, but the lessons I learned through the process were invaluable.

It was also this culture that resonated with me when the time came to start thinking where I wanted to go to work. And the "little creamery" was at the top of my list of hopeful employers.

At the end of the spring semester of my final year at Baylor, I reached back out to John Barnhill, hoping he remembered our time together with this earlier research project. This time the call was centered around returning to Brenham for the possibility of a job interview. I will never forget his immediate response: "Can you be here tomorrow at 10:00?" to which I replied, "Absolutely!" The interview must have gone well because six weeks later, John called with a job offer in the newly entered Dallas market. After prayerfully considering it, I called back a few days later and accepted. Having secured a job even before my last semester began sure took the pressure off those final months.

I graduated in December of 1980, then went straight to work in Dallas on January 1, 1981. My career would begin as a territory manager, whose responsibilities consisted of overseeing and managing a part of Blue Bell's selling area in that market. This included a variety of duties with the ultimate objective of taking care of the customer (the account) that would, in turn, take care of the consumer. This included making sure each account was properly serviced, along with introducing new items, obtaining additional space, and calling on new business. Even though we had been in the Dallas market since 1978, our growth was just beginning to explode.

In 1982, I relocated to the other side of the metroplex and became the assistant branch manager of the newly opened Fort Worth branch. It was so exciting to watch consumers become loyal fans by embracing our iconic flavors, such as Homemade Vanilla and Dutch Chocolate, as well as gravitating to our newest creation, Cookies 'n Cream. We became the correct answer to the trivia question, "Who was the first company to commercially package Cookies 'n Cream?"

The San Antonio market was next on our radar, and in 1984, I was asked to become branch manager of our newest branch. Returning to my hometown was a dream come true and finally being able to provide ice cream to all my friends and loved ones replaced my bragging of just how good the ice cream was.

I continued to watch Blue Bell take Texas by storm in the years ahead, and in 1989, the decision was made to cross the Texas border and venture into Oklahoma and Louisiana, expanding into Oklahoma

City and Baton Rouge. As more Americans learned about our ice cream, we continued to move into more states. Yet, with production capacity limits to match the explosive growth, our goal wasn't to try and become the number one brand in the country overnight. Instead, it was to offer the very best ice cream consistently in every market that we serviced. With that simple approach, national rankings would eventually take care of themselves.

From 1990 until 2014, our growth continued at a steady pace in both existing markets as well as new market entries. We weren't just in Texas anymore, and by the beginning of 2015, we were available in twenty-three states. Our territory had stretched from Arizona and Colorado, all across the southern part of the United States to Florida, then up the east coast to parts of Virginia. This footprint represented approximately 30 percent of the total ice cream market nationally, and according to A.C. Nielsen, our total ice cream sales placed us as one of the top two brands nationwide.

From only two gallons of ice cream a day back in 1911 to millions of gallons produced annually one hundred years later, we had become one of the nation's leading brands while only servicing about a third of the country. We were using milk from about 50,000 cows a day to make our tasty treats.

Momentum continued to build through 2015 as we were positioned for another outstanding year, including our latest new market entry: Las Vegas, Nevada.

But as exciting as the year appeared to be, things changed in a heartbeat when the phone rang on the night of February 13, 2015. A pathogen had been detected in certain Blue Bell products, potentially affecting not only our company, but the lives of each of our employees.

It's in those moments—moments of fear and uncertainty—you have to trust God's plan, especially when things just don't make sense. These moments also seem to be the place when you realize there is nothing more you can do except become totally dependent on God through faith. That's the place where fear tries to relentlessly take over, yet peace comes when faith begins.

Hours can turn into days, and possibly months or even years, but trusting gives way to allowing God to work for His glory.

> *And we know that God causes everything to work*
> *together for the good of those who love God and are*
> *called according to His purpose for them.*
>
> —ROMANS 8:28

Storms are going to come, and ours was about to arrive.

02

The Hunt

I can remember going hunting with my father as far back as when I was five years old. I wasn't sure about the hunting part but having one-on-one time with Dad was special, and I never wanted to pass up the opportunity when asked to go.

Even now, I love to hunt, and I have to admit just the sight of a Cabela's or Scheels Sporting Goods store can send my heart racing in incredible anticipation. If you didn't grow up hunting, don't worry. I promise there's something in this chapter for you too, because there are many things we can all learn by being still and surrounded by the splendor of God's creation. Especially out in the woods.

My wife prefers fishing and can fish me under the boat, but hunting will always be my favorite way to relax because it still brings up those good memories from going out in the woods with my family.

As a kid, spending time in the woods was always a great experience for my entire family—from hunting rabbits and squirrels to dove and quail hunting. Periodically, we would join my aunt, uncle, and cousin out on their deer lease, ready to shoot anything we legally could. The key was to always be ready, and if you didn't react immediately when spotting the potential prey, my aunt would jump up and accomplish the task before you could even blink. My aunt could shoot, which made it easy to obey her whenever she gave instructions!

Hearing the news that our family was going out to West Texas to try and harvest a whitetail deer was always the ultimate invite and most exciting of all hunts. A successful hunt for my dad and uncle meant bringing back enough deer meat for the freezer to last for the upcoming year. And, if you had ever had my mom's venison fried steak, you would understand how mouthwatering and motivating this challenge would be. For my cousin and me, it wasn't just the hunt that excited us, it was all about the blueberry pancakes at 4:30 in the morning, provided by the local motel for all hunters who stayed there. I don't remember the name of that hotel, but I sure remember the pancakes! There isn't much that would motivate me to get up at that hour, but for some reason, a plate of hot blueberry pancakes, dripping in melted butter and warm maple syrup, accompanied by a tall glass of ice-cold milk, was ten times louder than any alarm clock could ever be.

Looking back now as a father, I don't quite understand Mom and Dad's rationale for filling the stomachs of two young boys with a month's supply of sugar and then expecting us to sit quietly for hours in the woods. It didn't make any sense, but I never questioned it!

Going hunting with the family was a totally different experience than when it was just Dad and me. With Dad, it was usually sitting quietly for a few hours on the ground in a makeshift cedar log tree stand, waiting for the big buck to walk in. I remember it would require having a vivid imagination to occupy my mind during the idle time while sitting on the ground, not making a sound or even moving around very much. There were no iPhones or video games to keep me occupied, or even a *Johnny Quest* cartoon book to transport me to an even greater adventure. So, during those times, I resorted to drawing in the dirt with a small stick and just enjoyed being with Dad. Honestly, it was a safe place to be, especially in the woods.

With the whole family, it was a whole different adventure. After the shortened night of rest and a belly stuffed with the hotel's finest short stacks, we would set out. The ride from the hotel to the property was just long enough to mesmerize my cousin and me back to sleep, but once we turned off the highway asphalt onto the dirt road, we knew we were getting closer.

The next few miles were the hardest to get through for a few reasons. First, the anticipation—knowing we were getting close heightened our level of excitement. On the other hand, the final mile or two of dirt road felt more like the surface of the moon, every bump and turn resembling a wooden roller coaster ride from an amusement park. The craziness of these emotions made the experience that much better because soon we would be hunting. As the pancakes entered the spin cycle within my stomach, I wondered if this was how IHOP got its name. Finally, upon arriving at the camp house, we transferred all our gear into the limo of choice—an old, dust-filled jeep with a speedometer past its recording capabilities. It also had accommodations for four passengers inside and two up on the roof. Talk about a roller coaster.

Loaded down with an ice chest full of water and soft drinks, shopping bags full of sandwiches and snacks, we were ready for the adventure, and off we would go. My aunt, normally the skilled driver chosen to navigate our group over this mine-filled terrain, would settle behind the wheel while my mom would fall in the passenger seat. The kids would set up shop in the back seat, ready for action even though our view was limited. Located on the makeshift bench seat on top of the Jeep, my dad and uncle sat comfortably, or as much as the conditions would allow. These two world-renowned hunters (in my mind at least) positioned themselves in this luxurious penthouse suite, surrounded by what appeared to be a crash bar, which they used to balance their guns in the event a deer presented itself.

Once in place, off we would go, traveling the western Hill Country with one thing on all of our minds.

On those special family hunting trips, I don't actually remember if anyone ever shot a trophy buck, even though I know it wasn't for lack of trying. But what I do remember is the time we spent together as a family and making the most of each adventure. Yes, the goal was the hunt, but stepping away from the world to be with family was so much more meaningful than the hunt itself. It was the journey (and perhaps the pancakes).

Just like in our everyday lives, mountaintop views are spectacular, and yet, the quick majestic view seems short-lived compared to the journey it took to get there. On the other hand, when in the valley, time seems to linger forever. Ironically, it's also where we find our strength to push on and where we learn what we're made of and made *for*. As much as I cherish the most exciting moments in my life, it's the struggles that have made me who I am today, and I wouldn't change that for anything in the world.

As fun and exciting as those family trips were, the older I became, I realized there was nothing like those special times when it was just Dad and me. It wasn't necessarily the conversation between us, which usually consisted of me asking a barrage of endless "why" questions, but just time being with him. As I got older, it became the perfect time to discuss "life" and absorb what seemed to be an endless amount of knowledge and wisdom that always seemed to be on target with the advice I needed to hear. Then there were times when neither one of us spoke, and I would sit, resting in the security of the quietness that brought such peace. Dad had a way of loving you, even in the quietest of moments.

I can't help thinking that's exactly what God desires for each of us. To get one-on-one with the Creator of the universe and ask Him the toughest of "why" questions, to pray for others, but most importantly, rest in the silence of His great and mighty power. No matter the issue, it is always a safe place to retreat and find peace. In fact, it's the most important place.

Some of the most memorable trips came in those impressionable years, and the life lessons have left a legacy that I still refer back to, sixty years later.

I remember early on that while traveling to the property, Dad would always go over the usual rules of hunting. He would stress the importance of staying close together and being quiet. As a young child, the latter didn't make a lot of sense, but I was willing to learn. He would whisper softly over and over the same phrase, "As we make our way out to the deer stand, stay as close to me as you can, and be ever so quiet. Unless it's an emergency, do not talk." Even though there weren't any blueberry pancakes involved, I was still determined to follow the instructions given to me as best I could so I could reserve an opportunity for the next outing if things went well.

After arriving at the property in the darkness before morning light, Dad would gather all the necessary equipment, including his gun, ammunition, and flashlight, and off we would go. The instructions again were simple: stay close and be as quiet as possible. Right?

The walk from the car to the deer stand was probably no more than twenty minutes, but when you're five years old and it's pitch black all around you, it seems like eternity. "Stay close and be as quiet as possible" meant I had to focus on every step, yet the unfamiliar sounds of the woods fought for my attention. Each rustling of the leaves in the trees or hoot from the local owl began to remind me of the same fear I had at night in my bedroom once the light was turned off. These newly discovered distractions immediately shifted my focus, and within seconds, Dad would inevitably turn around and repeat the same command. "Be quiet and stay right behind me!" O.K., I'll try better this time, I'd think, and we'd continue on.

It didn't take long for me to realize that each step my dad took paved the way to achieving his goal. Somehow, someway, he knew where to walk. And if I could somehow step in the same spot, any potential twig or leaf would have already been broken or smashed down, leaving a tested path for my little feet to follow. Then, I noticed that my dad's flashlight only illuminated one step at a time. To be as quiet as I could, each step required serious concentration. Even though I was being stretched from one step to the next, this newfound strategy seemed to be paying dividends, and it wasn't long before we reached our destination.

It's amazing to find a new peace when I move in the direction God would have me walk.

Like following behind my dad, following in the footsteps that Jesus has prepared for me requires the same amount of concentration and trust in order to live a Christ-filled life to the fullest. The problem is that I start each day with good intentions to walk where God is leading, but just like young me in the woods, the distractions of the world are always vying for my attention. I get easily sidetracked, and inevitably, I stumble off the safe path that God has provided. The beauty of our Father is that His love for us and His overwhelming grace allows us to recalculate our compass and try again. I can almost hear in a deep and powerful voice ... *recalculating*!

STORMS AHEAD

Back at Blue Bell, on February 13, 2015, my early lessons on trusting God and concentrating on following in His footsteps were about to be tested. So often, the only way we can see His light is when we follow close to Him, trusting as we focus on each step that we take. Listening to His voice, walking in His light, and trusting no matter how difficult, each step of the way. And when my phone rang that Friday evening, I was ready to take the next steps.

03

In Plain Sight

The year 1969 was memorable for a lot of reasons. Neil Armstrong took one small step onto the surface of the moon, Willie Mays of the San Francisco Giants became only the second player in Major League Baseball to hit six hundred career home runs, and I experienced my first kiss on top of our church roof. The relationship lasted about as long as the kiss, especially when I found out the meaning of cooties. It was already a monumental year, and Christmas was still around the corner! I was pumped. As a nine-and-a-half-year-old boy, Christmas was the most exciting day of the year. Birthdays were great, but there was something uniquely special about Christmas that you didn't experience any other time of the year. The weeks before this special day, I would camp out on the floor with my head immersed in the toy section of the Sears and Roebuck catalog, looking for that perfect gift. This particular Christmas was no different from the few I had experienced before, so the journey began. It was going to be hard to beat the Hot Wheel car set I'd received the previous year, but I was up for the challenge.

As I navigated past the Rock 'Em Sock 'Em Robots and G.I. Joe action figures, I landed on a really cool kids toolbox, complete with an assortment of tools. For reasons I can't remember, the decision was made, and the anticipation phase commenced. If I had only known then that home repairs would not be my gift, the Rock 'Em Sock 'Em Robot would be a more entertaining present.

As thrilling as Christmas Day was, Christmas Eve was just the opposite. Time seemed to slow to a crawl, and the excitement left me waking up at all hours of the night, thinking morning would never come—but then it did. With strict instructions to stay in my room until the word was given, the anticipation was more than I could bear until finally it was time. As I ran into the living room, I quickly noticed the tree and everything around it looked as it did the night before. Where are the presents? Had we been robbed? Collectively, between my older sister and two younger brothers, we knew there had been some mistake. No gifts, seriously? Maybe Santa was running behind, or even worse, maybe we were all on the naughty list. That made more sense to my younger brothers and me, but my sister? No way. She was an angel.

As panic went into overdrive, Dad proceeded to point out the specially wrapped aluminum cans under the tree. With a new sense of curiosity, we each found our very own personalized can, decorated and complete with our name on it. What was this, I thought. Possibly a can of corn, green beans, or (worse yet) spinach? Upon further inspection, each had its own design and, if shaken, seemed to have rocks or pebbles inside, giving it extra weight. A lump of coal for each of the Dickson kids ... never ... right? To settle our disappointment, Dad assisted each of us in opening our cans, one at a time. The suspense was even worse than the annual ripping of the paper from years past. How in the world could they fit a toolbox in a can?

One by one, we took turns opening our treasured can, only to find detailed instructions that led us on our very own scavenger hunt through the house! Going from one mystery location to another with Mom and Dad's assistance, we followed the instructions to each spot until, eventually, it brought us back into the room in which we started. To our surprise, our presents had been there all along, unwrapped and in plain view.

For me, my new toolbox was positioned on the lower shelf, right next to the Christmas tree, and my sister's necklace hung on a branch on the tree itself, in plain sight for each of us to see. The problem was, we were looking for presents, so we overlooked the obvious.

I still think about that unique Christmas and how "Santa" made it an extra special experience for each of us. It also reminded us to pay attention to the many blessings surrounding us on a daily basis—not only those in plain sight but also those that needed to be unwrapped. They are right in front of us; we just have to be looking for them.

I SPY

Another great example of my parents incorporating "looking for blessings" techniques came when we took family vacations. If you have ever traveled more than two city blocks from home, you can relate to the "I'm over this road vacation" experience. Each trip as a family can reveal a special bonding time, yet the challenge any parent faces requires a ton of patience, mixed with a variety of top-notch parental skills.

The last ring of the school bell serves as the starting gun for this summer bonanza of activities, indicating summertime is officially here. As exciting as this last day of school is for children, parents know the next ten to twelve weeks revolve around an assortment of carpooling trips and summer activities. Wedged in there somewhere is the long-anticipated family vacation. Whether it's a few days of staycation at a nearby campground or a full-blown trip to Disney World, there is nothing like it. Taking a break from the day-to-day routine also meant creating memories, good or not-so-good, no matter the destination. Memories that would last a lifetime.

Growing up with two younger brothers and a slightly older sister meant my summer vacation reflections would develop looking through the rear window of our beautiful emerald-green Rambler station wagon. For those reminiscing with me, this was the one that sported the stylish woodgrain panels down both sides of a slick station wagon design and a rooftop luggage rack that would accommodate the multitude of suitcases for our family of six.

My preferred "spot" was always the rear-facing pull-out seat in the very back of the car. Move over, spare tire; I'm setting up shop! From there, I felt I had the best view of where we'd been and freedom from distress calls of "Stop touching me!" or "You're on my side!" for the duration of the trip. When compared to the second row, I believed my independent oasis was the best. However, over time, I realized that doing so meant I was the last one to see what others had already experienced. This was especially true when the questions shifted from "Are we there yet?" and "I need to go to the bathroom!" to Mom saying, "What games can we play?" Now, for those of you who are younger, you must remember iPhones and portable DVD players were years from being invented, so imagination became your best friend as you traveled down the highway.

We would always start with the conventional games to occupy our time, like "ABC" and "Beaver Cleaver," but as you can imagine, playing from the back seat was a lot like eating leftovers. It was great at first, but all the good letters on signs were taken before they appeared in full view from my position. Either way, we all would eventually lose interest.

In its absence, Dad would have us fixated in each car window, trying to spot a deer or two. As good as we thought we might be, he seemed to always win at this game. Even so, we all took turns staring into the woods to find any resemblance to this prized animal. I can still hear Dad saying, "Look for what doesn't belong, what stands out in the scenery or looks different. Once you see it, it's hard to unsee it." It took practice, but to this day, I enjoy that same challenge, and the memories make for a double blessing. I also wonder what the world would see if they were to play the same game, yet looking for Christians. Not to judge, but I wonder, if they played "I Spy the Christian," what would that look like? Observing what we say, our attitude, or our actions, would they be able to spot those who love Christ? Do we stand out or blend into the scenery?

The tricky part is that we are to live in the world but not of the world. His light should shine through us and not center on us. As the moon reflects the sun, we should also reflect the *Son*.

Over two thousand years ago, many were looking for a King—the promised one who would come and save the world. As they looked in all the places they expected He would appear, they looked right past the manger and missed the prophecy's promise altogether.

For to us a child is born,
to us a son is given,
and the government will be on his shoulders.

And he will be called
Wonderful Counselor, Mighty God,
Everlasting Father, Prince of Peace.

—ISAIAH 9:6

I have often wondered how they missed it. Yet, when looking for something or someone in the wrong place, there's a good chance you will miss it, too. It reminds me of the story I once heard of a gentleman searching underneath a streetlight at night for a valuable ring he had lost. While searching, a policeman walked up and asked him what he was doing. He frantically replied that he had lost a valuable ring that had been in his family for generations and was trying to find it. The policeman politely asks, "About where did you lose it?" to which the man replies, "Down the road a ways." Confused by his answer, the officer asks, "Why, then, are you looking for it here?" to which the man said, "Because this is where the light is."

Unfortunately, when Christ was born, many people were casually waiting for the Messiah or not looking at all. Ironically, if they were to follow the light, they would have found the Savior. Instead, they failed to see the radiant star bright in the night sky. Rather, they went on their way with their busy schedule, complacent to their surroundings, and remained in the dark while *thinking* they were in the light. The problem was that they were looking in all the wrong places. Artificial, man-made light will do that. The shiniest objects that reflect this world will always disappoint. They also looked past the prophetic scriptures that were left by our Heavenly Father for them to see. Humbly, in a manger, taking on the form of mankind, Jesus entered the world. Even though they had the sight to see, they lived unaware that the King of Kings was now among them.

"The tricky part is that we are to live in the world but not of the world. His light should shine through us and not centered on us. As the moon reflects the sun, we should also reflect the Son."

Look for what doesn't belong! Even if you can see, you can be blinded by what's right in front of you. To emphasize this thought, you would have to close your eyes. Of all the "senses" we are blessed with, it's hard to imagine a world without sight.

Then there is Helen Keller. Helen Keller lost her eyesight and hearing at the young age of nineteen months old. Ironically, what seemed to be a terrible twist of fate didn't slow her down. In fact, she probably lived a more fulfilling life than most of us will ever imagine. One of her more profound quotes encapsulates this life surrounded by darkness. Helen once said, "The only thing worse than being born blind is having sight but no vision." For some, what seems so clear and vivid is totally missed by others.

> **"The only thing worse than being born blind is having sight but no vision."**
> **—Helen Keller**

Another person with this kind of vision is Andrea Bocelli, one of the greatest Italian tenors ever to sing. Since 1992, his music has captivated audiences all over the world, singing both classical and pop music for all generations. What many don't know is that Andrea was born with congenital glaucoma and, at the age of twelve, became completely blind due to the illness. He was hit in the eye during a soccer match and experienced a brain hemorrhage. Doctors tried everything to save his eyesight yet were unsuccessful. Even though this news was devastating, it didn't stop Andrea from pushing forward with his music. His voice became the window into a world we could only dream about. To date, he has recorded over fifteen solo albums, three of which were greatest hits, and nine operas, selling over seventy-five million records worldwide. His powerful, soul-penetrating voice mesmerizes his audience and leaves them wanting more after each and every song.

Recently, when visiting my sister in San Antonio, she shared Andrea's latest duet with his son Matteo. Her excitement was filled with tears of joy, and the message behind the music had penetrated her heart. As I listened to the words, I was also transported into an imaginary world. I felt like I was given a small glimpse of what it must have been like to walk in total darkness, then, with childlike faith, become totally dependent on my Heavenly Father's light to guide each step.

I wish you could put this book down at this moment and listen to this magnificent song, "Fall on Me," to capture this true experience.

Fear can take you places you don't want to go to and at times leave you in total darkness. It's in those moments you must look past the manger and look to the cross. With His arms open wide, Jesus says fall on me no matter where you are, and feel my presence everywhere. Breathe in the love of Christ and rest. Journey to the place where peace passes all logic and understanding, no matter the circumstances. For His love is right there at the tree, with arms stretched out wide ….

…. In plain sight.

04

Chinese Bamboo Tree

O n the morning of June 15, 1987, I received a call from our home office in Brenham, Texas. Normally it was our district manager, Steve James, calling to get an update on current events at our branch. Steve was also my direct supervisor, and checking in was routine. On this particular morning, though, it was John Barnhill, our executive vice president and general sales manager, on the other line.

It was always great to hear from John. From our initial time spent during the interview process to those special occasions when he visited our branch, John seemed to have a way of challenging you as a leader as well as a salesman, yet always with words of encouragement. He was also a master at marketing and had a keen eye for the branding of products. Especially ours! Projecting the right image was as critical for our company as well as our ice cream, and every detail in the process mattered. From our iconic "cow and girl" logo to the phrase "fresh from the little creamery in Brenham," John played a key role in the development of every detail.

It wasn't unusual for John to periodically call to check in on our progress in the market and ask about our employees, but the topic of this particular call was far from normal. After the brief branch update, John asked me to shut my office door so he could discuss a confidential opportunity. The brief journey to oblige allowed my imagination to kick into overdrive, and I returned with a rush of anticipation.

John had been instrumental in my transfer from Fort Worth to San Antonio back in 1984, including my promotion to branch manager. It was also a huge vote of confidence, and I didn't want to let him down. At twenty-four years old, married with one young daughter and a second one on the way, I was literally on top of the world.

Within the first few years there, our family settled into a new home, became very active in church, and I became a member of the Downtown Optimist Club, where both my dad and grandfather were members. We were set for the long haul and ready to grow as a family, as well as become the market leader with our ice cream.

Our branch (or distribution center) in San Antonio was the eighth to open for the company since 1960. Consumers in central Texas immediately embraced the love of Homemade Vanilla, Cookies 'n Cream, and all our other flavors as much as the previous seven.

For me, it was the opportunity of a lifetime to return not just to my hometown but to work approximately three miles from where I grew up. But just as I settled into my comfortable and familiar surroundings, God's direction for my life shifted, and it was delivered through this pivotal phone call.

So, that June morning, John's call was met with an immediate mixture of emotions. Senior management had determined that, in order to grow as a company, we would need to either expand our production capacity in Brenham or build an additional plant somewhere in or just outside our current service area.

The discussion of a new plant was exciting, but I was confused about how it involved me. He went on to share that with the addition of a new plant, there would be a new sales territory outside of Texas for future expansion, as well as the ability to provide ice cream to our current markets as sales continued to increase.

Finally, he revealed Blue Bell would be crossing state lines and entering the Oklahoma market in two phases: a branch in Oklahoma City in 1989, then a manufacturing plant in Broken Arrow (just outside of Tulsa) in 1992. The heart of the call came when John asked, "Would you be willing to leave San Antonio at the end of 1988 and move to Oklahoma to open the branch in Oklahoma City?" but before I could gather any words to respond, he followed with "then move to Broken Arrow to open the Tulsa/Broken Arrow market?"

He explained that the request came with the potential of being promoted to district manager (now titled regional manager) and overseeing all branch operations in Oklahoma and future markets in the surrounding states. Phone calls have played a key role in my life, and this one I was sure I would never forget. I told him, "I would definitely have to discuss the offer with my family, along with praying for direction in my decision."

As exciting as this opportunity seemed to be, our decision came with a price. For me, it was especially difficult because San Antonio was home. Period. My young family had adapted to our new environment, and had become involved in many activities and developed new friendships. So, do I stay comfortable now that I'm back at home, or walk by faith and move to a location where neither of us knows anyone? It was equally exciting to be a part of this pivotal and historical time in our company's history.

Staying in San Antonio also meant we would be not only close to my parents, who provided much-needed babysitting services, but also to remain close with both of my two brothers and sister and their families. It was not unusual for us to meet together at a restaurant for dinner on a Friday night or just pick up dinner and head to Mom and Dad's house. Mom would always throw a cake or pie together while we visited and top it off with none other than Blue Bell. As a close-knit family, we were fortunate that we all got along and loved being together. This tradition would come to an end if we were to move up north. The ultimate was attending church where all our children could grow up together, both physically and spiritually.

Blue Bell would need an answer quickly in order to make other plans in the event I declined, but a decision like this needed to be thought out and prayed over. The most difficult part of the request was that I was unable to discuss it with anyone other than my wife since our entry into Oklahoma was confidential, and the move was still a year and a half away. Saying yes would almost put a hold on any personal plans we might have had, yet now, with three small children under the age of seven, it seemed to be a good opportunity to at least consider. Over the course of the next few weeks, my wife and I discussed the pros and cons, then prayed earnestly for God's will in our direction. At times like this, I earnestly pray for peace in the decision, then once I sense His direction, I try hard to walk by faith.

If I left, was I walking by faith for my own benefit, or should I decline the request and stay for my family's benefit and comfort in our familiar surroundings? More importantly, which path was going to glorify God the most through obedience? Probably the toughest part of walking *by faith* is discerning which path is right. Either option before us could be justified, and with pure heart, God would bless us either way. But finding peace in the decision required a relationship with our Father, and the closer the walk, the clearer His voice would be.

The gift of "choice" can be difficult, to say the least.

Promotions that come with a title or a stature can make things pretty foggy too when seeking His will. Having trust in where He calls you can be difficult when there are so many unknowns.

After much prayer and deliberation, I accepted the offer. Leaving the comforts of home would not be easy, but I knew He would guide our steps in this journey. I also remembered how God had led me to Baylor, then to Blue Bell, and I believed He had more plans for me and my family, if we just trusted Him with this leap of faith.

As planned, the opening of the Oklahoma City branch happened in the spring of 1989, and for the first time since opening our doors in 1907, consumers outside of Texas could buy Blue Bell serviced by a local branch. As for our family, we settled in a rented house in Norman and began adjusting to a new life—making new friends with neighbors and those at church.

What made the move especially difficult was that we knew our time in Oklahoma City would be temporary once the OKC market was established. We would then move to Broken Arrow, Oklahoma, where our manufacturing plant would soon be built. It's hard to establish yourself in a new location, especially knowing you won't be there long.

On February 27, 1989, we began delivering our products to supermarkets, convenience stores, ice cream parlors, and restaurants across central Oklahoma. With our entry, word quickly spread, and the public began demanding Blue Bell in the Tulsa area. A newfound excitement about "the little creamery" immediately spread throughout the state, and word of a new plant added to the excitement.

Consumer demand has always been our greatest ally, and with their strong request for Blue Bell, we opened a temporary facility the following year in Broken Arrow, two years ahead of schedule. This decision meant moving to Broken Arrow earlier than anticipated, but it also meant my family could begin permanently settling into our new community.

So, by the spring of 1990, Blue Bell ice cream was available in most of Oklahoma. As we began to settle into this new life, things seemed really good. Yet, any discussion of me becoming a new regional manager of a newly formed region had become nonexistent. I believed I was following God's voice when moving to Oklahoma, but the silence drowned out any excitement about what was taking place.

The discussion of a promotion finally came, but not in the way I had anticipated.

As impatient as I had become, my anxiety quickly shifted to eagerness when I was asked to meet with my immediate supervisors, Melvin Ziegenbein and John Barnhill, after dinner at one of our corporate outings. Finally! This was it. What I had been waiting for, and the main reason I had moved from Texas to Oklahoma, was finally coming to fruition. Looking back now, it was apparent that my focus had shifted from God's will to Ricky's will.

After dinner, Melvin caught my attention and directed me to a side room where we could discuss these future plans.

Or so I thought.

I could tell from entering the room that the mood was not one of celebration. In fact, it felt just the opposite. The level of energy that filled the restaurant seemed to melt faster than a scoop of ice cream on a summer day. I could tell by their demeanor that this wasn't going to be a night of celebration, and my intuition was confirmed quickly. The three of us sat down at the table, and for the next thirty minutes, the discussion was centered more on my performance than that of any promotional praise.

On a page and a half, single-spaced white notepad, Melvin went through a list of things I should be giving attention to, as well as things I needed to work on, in order to perform like the manager they had seen in the past. My thoughts and emotions went through the roof. Were they right? How did I get so far off track? I sat and listened to the review, trying not to argue their points. Sitting quietly while being criticized isn't easy, but listening instead of reacting defensively is always the better choice. Instead, I began to listen intently to their evaluation in order to get focused on where I needed to be.

After the meeting, I returned to my hotel room frustrated and angry. What was supposed to be a meeting centered around my accomplishments and leadership skills had just turned into a downhome brutal critique with me at center stage. I remember sitting on the bed and saying out loud, "Why God? Why did you bring me to Oklahoma? Why did you ask me to move my family away from Texas and my extended family, not just once but twice, from Oklahoma City to Broken Arrow?"

As I said those last words, I felt God's voice pick up right where Melvin's and John's had left off. Not in an audible voice, but His words went straight to my soul, saying, "You're not here for you, you're here for me. You're here to do my will, not yours, no matter what that looks like. Let go of the titles and focus on the mission. By doing so, you will glorify me, and you will have peace." Talk about a double whammy and a true reality check! Even though I believed moving to Oklahoma was in His will, it had become apparent to everyone that after I arrived, I began to drift from center, focusing on me and not what truly mattered.

At that moment, in that hotel room, I realized I had to make a life-changing decision. Am I going to get mad and walk out? Am I going to complain that I was misled by coming to Oklahoma, or am I going to get back on my knees and listen to God's direction for my life, no matter the assignment?

I chose the latter, and that decision changed my life.

Within the next few years, our company went through a management realignment, and I was asked to become general manager of our Broken Arrow plant. After seventeen years of selling the best ice cream in the country, I was going to get a peek behind the freezer door and get ringside seats on how it's produced. Talk about taking me out of my comfort zone. I had been taught the basics of how ice cream was made, but to actually manage a plant would stretch me in more ways than I could ever imagine.

As exciting as this "new" position seemed to be, I recognized its challenges, and even more alarming, accepting the position meant I would be giving up the plans to grow in the sales department. I had been praying for God's will, but this opportunity sure didn't line up with my plans. Had there been a mistake? Is this the reason I moved from San Antonio? Then I remembered my conversation with God. "You're not here for you; you're here for me."

Trust is critical, even when it doesn't make sense.

So, even though someone else would be promoted to the position I had moved to Oklahoma for, I had tremendous peace that I was right where God had placed me—all for His glory and not mine. What I couldn't see at the time was God used those years from 1996 until 2003 to expose me to the production side of our operations and give me knowledge I would have never obtained had I had it my way. That knowledge also prepared me for what was to come. I am so thankful I embraced the opportunity God had given me instead of resisting it.

I carried those evaluation notes in my briefcase for years and made a habit of referring back to them on occasion to keep me centered. Invest in your employees, know your customers, provide the best possible service to each account, and support them consistently with the best ice cream "in the country," to name a few. These critical review points kept me centered on our mission as a company, instead of on my own desires. These were steps that made Blue Bell unique with not just the freshest product but also as a company providing each account with the best possible service. I have often heard it said that it's our employees who are the most important ingredient when defining our success, and I firmly believe it. It's great to have goals and dreams, but in order to reach them, you must stay in the moment and be the best you can be, no matter the job or task.

The most recited prayer in our Christian faith is The Lord's Prayer, which includes the words, "Thy will be done." Four of the most powerful yet difficult words to say in any circumstance. We might be ready to die for Christ, but are we willing to live for Him? It's a daily decision. Don't get me wrong, I fight this battle each and every day, and the fine line between confidence and pride is very thin. We need to go boldly, using the talents that God has given us, but we must be humble in our approach, letting our praise for each opportunity go upward instead of inward.

If there is a scripture that encapsulates these instructions, it is found in Romans 12:1–3 (NIV):

Therefore, I urge you, brothers and sisters, in view of God's mercy, to offer your bodies as a living sacrifice, holy and pleasing to God— this is your true and proper worship. ² Do not conform to the pattern of this world, but be transformed by the renewing of your mind. Then you will be able to test and approve what God's will is—his good, pleasing and perfect will. ³ For by the grace given me I say to every one of you: Do not think of yourself more highly than you ought, but rather think of yourself with sober judgment, in accordance with the faith God has distributed to each of you.

I saw firsthand the grip of this thing called "pride" and was unaware of it settling in and taking over through this experience. What started with good intent eroded through pride's disguise, taking me off the path that God had planned for me.

Another example of this can be found in how we use our cell phone or navigation device in our cars. We plug in where we want to go then take off, listening to the directions that were programmed in order to get us to our destination. The problem that I have found is, while I start off with good intentions, I tend to see alternative routes that I think will save time and venture away from the predetermined path. Inevitably, I end up lost or find that it took longer to get back to where I originally planned to go. When I think of God's will for my life, there have been times I have become fearful of the path or direction He is asking me to take, allowing doubt to creep in and set up shop in my mind. From moving from one city to another or shifting from my sales position and running a production plant, obedience can be difficult.

My concern centers around the unknown potential outcome or the length of time it will take to get there. The simplest way to dissolve this fear is to trust. I have found that the more I trust, the more peace I receive, even when things don't make sense.

The fear of letting go and trusting also requires patience. More times than not, God's timing takes a lot longer than our timing, and if I'm not careful, I become complacent in the direction I am supposed to go. Throughout each of our lives, there will be many breathtaking moments as we enjoy the mountain tops. Our wedding day, the birth of a child, or the first taste of Homemade Vanilla, to name a few. (O.K.

I had to throw that one in for fun.) There will also be valleys that will come upon us unexpectedly that will drive us to our knees. The unexpected news of a medical test or the loss of a loved one. You might find yourself in a situation you never thought could be possible and fear strikes your soul, leaving you asking more questions of God than you can ever imagine. Found in the heart of the most familiar Psalm, we find hope in these moments of despair.

> *Even though I walk through the valley of the shadow of death,*
> *For YOU ARE WITH ME:*
> *Your rod and your staff. They comfort me.*

> —PSALM 23: 4

It's what we do as we climb the mountain that prepares us for either the mountain top or valley experience. While on our journey, if we're not careful, we can fall into complacency. We start our journey with good intentions, but over time begin to rely on our own abilities, leaving God out of our daily routine. When it seems that nothing is happening during the journey, remember Romans 8:28 that says so clearly:

> *And we know that for those who love God all things work together*
> *for good, for those who are called according to His purpose.*

Walking in God's will can look and even feel strange, but knowing you are there for His glory, provides an incredible peace.

A great example of waiting on God's timing can be found in the growth pattern of the Chinese bamboo tree. It has been said that the Chinese bamboo tree can grow over ninety feet tall, with the tallest tree ever recorded coming in at 130 feet. It is one of the hardest materials, with strength greater than steel, yet safe to eat. The most amazing thing about the Chinese bamboo tree is it takes up to five years to break the surface of the ground, but once it does, it grows over ninety feet in a matter of five weeks. In one day, it can grow up to thirty-five inches at a rate of 1.5 inches per hour.

In order to survive and grow to such heights, it must be watered and fertilized every day for five years. So, one might ask the question, does it take five weeks or five years to grow? And the answer is yes! If we surrender our hearts to Christ and water and cultivate our daily journey with the master, we can accomplish mighty things according to His will. To do so, we must turn off our pride meter and turn on our Father's navigational system to guide us each step of the way.

As strong and tall as the Chinese Bamboo tree becomes when nourished properly, it also requires a tremendous amount of patience. Just think: If a bamboo tree can grow that much in just five weeks after growing under the ground for five years, just think how much we can grow when planted and nourished in God's word. Knowing that no matter how much time it takes, it's in His perfect timing and our obedience that His will can be done.

I truly believe moving to Oklahoma was all in God's timing, and I also believe it was His timing to position me in the plant in Broken Arrow, even when it didn't make sense. It just took a good old-fashioned stern evaluation for me to get focused back on His purpose and not my desires. When you think God's timing is off, maybe it's because you're not ready. But no matter what, growing in Christ means trusting and knowing that He is still in control and that He is preparing you for what's to come. And yes, even if it doesn't make sense. The Refiner's fire can be incredibly uncomfortable, but He is making you into His masterpiece through the process, all to bring Him glory!

² Dear brothers and sisters, when troubles of any kind come your way, consider it an opportunity for great joy. ³ For you know that when your faith is tested, your endurance has a chance to grow. ⁴ So let it grow, for when your endurance is fully developed, you will be perfect and complete, needing nothing.

—JAMES 1:2-4

05

Monster Slide

In the spring of 1992, the first production lines outside Brenham, Texas began making ice cream. Key personnel had transferred from Brenham to operate the plant, and approximately 150 employees joined the Blue Bell family. It was also the first time for me to actually work at a location where our ice cream was produced. Talk about tempting. As rewarding as it is to enjoy a bowl of one of our many favorite flavors, there is nothing, and I mean nothing, like eating ice cream fresh from the production line. You talk about a land flowing with milk and honey …

The taste of ice cream before it has been hard frozen explodes with amazing flavor. Fresh milk, cream, sugar, and the freshest fruits combine the most ultimate experience one can possibly have. To take it to the ultimate experience, Homemade Vanilla right off the line will take you straight back to the Garden of Eden or, better yet, Heaven itself.

As mentioned in the previous chapter, in 1996, our Broken Arrow plant manager left the company to return to Brenham to take over the family business. With that open position, I moved from the sales department and became general manager of the plant. My sales and marketing background meant that I never anticipated being asked to run a manufacturing facility. All I knew about making ice cream was to "make sure you keep cranking until Mom says stop."

To say yes would also mean leaving the comforts of the sales side, but I recognized His voice in the decision, and with it came a strong peace! In the days that followed (even with that peace), I am not sure who was more concerned in this decision: me or my employees. I will never forget the faces of the staff members when I broke the news to them. As calmly as I could be, I remember explaining to the department heads that I was assuming the role of general manager. Immediately, the air seemed to leave the room, as did the color on each of their faces.

After a few seconds, which seemed like hours, I assured them that I wasn't there to make the ice cream. They knew how to do that and did it well. I was there to keep the ship going in the right direction.

I am sure I felt on the inside the same as they looked on the outside, but slowly, they began to accept my new role, and this new journey began.

Over the next six years, I poured myself into the plant's employees, realizing my limitations and knowledge of how ice cream was produced. They continued to make the "best ice cream in the country" (and even in "the city," for that matter), and my focus remained on working with each area, encouraging them to be the best they could be.

The experience was incredible, yet challenging. The first thing I learned was that managing employees in production required a different approach than managing those in sales. Many production employees were skilled at the technical side of operations, but managing people didn't come as naturally, whereas those in sales were more people-driven. Both are critical to success, and I found the common denominator came down to listening and caring.

I am a firm believer in servant leadership, and if at all possible, I want to be able to not only sympathize but empathize with their daily responsibilities. I have often heard it said, "All of us are smarter than one of us," and together we can accomplish anything. When they know you listen and, even more importantly, care, they become part of the solution. Talk about rewarding!

"A" FOR EFFORT

I will never forget my first day as general manager. I wanted so badly to jump in and be a part of the team, yet I knew I was extremely limited in what I could or should attempt, but I was determined to at least try. So, I worked my way down to the production floor, grabbed a smock, hair net, and ear plugs, washed my hands, and entered the production floor. Fortunately, I was greeted warmly by those in the room, yet they were probably more surprised at my visit than excited to see me. I cautiously made my way to the production floor and then over to the first operation.

On most days, half gallons of Homemade Vanilla were normally being produced, and today was no exception. The team of operators and packagers were working effortlessly together to ensure each half gallon was ready for the consumer. As easy as the continuous pace of each half gallon seemed to come down the line, trying to package four half gallons into a sleeve at a rate of fifty plus per minute was too intimidating to me. Potentially one day, yet not today, so I decided to keep moving.

As I approached the second operation, I immediately ruled out any personal involvement. The operation seemed complicated due to the speed, and a bad first impression would be disastrous. We were producing three-ounce tab lid cups for schools at a pace too fast to count. They would then put them into two stacks and push them into a paper bag, two dozen at a time. The bag was then taped shut, ready for the journey to their final destination. The employees were masters of their craft, and, thankfully, I chose to keep my distance. Visiting and encouraging everyone was one thing, but leaving the packaging to the professionals was the wise choice.

As I approached the third operation, my spirits jumped through the roof. Finally, an operation I think I can contribute to! (Or so I thought.) Here we were making sherbet quarts in plastic containers. The speed of each quart being filled seemed manageable, then they were stacked, one on top of the other. The final step was to put three stacks of quarts in a box, tape it, then send it to the deep freeze. The dream position I had been searching for was right in front of me, and I was ready to accept its challenge. I'm not necessarily known for my packing abilities, but I got this, and I was ready to get engaged. I thought, *All I have to do is fill the box, tape, and send.* Simple!

And with that, I walked up to Diana, my newly elected "employee of the month" (in my eyes, anyway), introduced myself, and then told her she was free to take an extra fifteen-minute break. I was there to relieve her. Not really sure what to think, she hesitated for a second, then stepped out of the way. Before the offer could be rescinded, she smiled and walked away. As she left, I reminded her of the fifteen minutes I had rewarded her. I was confident, but only to a point.

I immediately stepped into place, grabbed the first box and off I went, sliding the first pair of quarts into place, followed by the second. I then taped the box shut and placed it onto the conveyor, thinking that it was the best taped box in the history of mankind. I continued to watch the box, wondering when the sales employee on the other end of the process took this box out at the store, they would have to pause and recognize this amazing job.

After the brief reflection, I turned back to start my second box, only to realize there were now six boxes waiting for their amazing journey to begin. Well, lets say the next fourteen-and-a-half minutes were a nightmare, all to the amazement and entertainment of those I was working with. The chaos was similar to the *I Love Lucy* episode at the chocolate factory, only I couldn't just start eating the product to slow the process down.

After what seemed like an eternity, Diana finally returned to relieve me of total embarrassment and whispered in my ear, "Thank you," as if to give me an "A" for my effort. For years after that day, I made it a point to visit with each employee as I walked the floor, but I left the trained professionals to do their jobs. Believe me, they were thankful.

As much as I treasured those years in the plant, when I was asked to move to Brenham to become the general sales manager for the company, needless to say, I was humbled beyond measure.

Reflecting back over all the years that had passed from leaving San Antonio to that very moment, everything seemed to come into focus and how God had prepared me for this moment in time. Little did I know, He wasn't finished!

They say you never forget how to ride a bike; well, returning to the sales department brought me back to a place I was familiar with. It was a dream job, to say the least. Working directly for the vice president of sales, my responsibilities included overseeing the sales and marketing department, as well as advertising and public relations. It also included being a part of the flavor and product development team ... and yes, this included testing new flavors. Those were always fun days at the office.

This process started with recommendations from our research and development team, our employees, and customer creations. It is truly amazing the number of ways you can blend ingredients together and turn them into masterpieces. Through the process, some suggestions taste fantastic but can't be mass-produced to achieve the same results. On the other hand, other ideas are better left in the kitchen they were created in. Just saying ... but at least they tried. After narrowing down the field of contenders, our research and development team, along with our sales team, go to work to create what we hope is the next Cookies 'n Cream or Cookie Two Step. It's a tough job, but someone has to do it.

Besides testing the newest flavor creations, evaluating new market potential was equally rewarding.

To venture into a new territory and witness firsthand consumers trying our unique flavors for the first time always brought such joy. No matter how young or old you might be, when you're eating ice cream, it always seems to brighten your day. Over the years, after finding our way out of Texas, we tried to move across the country at a manageable pace. Making each flavor taste the same consistently is extremely important, and if you try to grow too fast, you can potentially compromise this process. It also seems that every market has its own personality and cultural foundations. It's fun to see which flavors a community embraces and which ones are left for others to try.

If you studied the growth strategy of Blue Bell ice cream over the past sixty-five years, you'd see a "cinch by the inch" philosophy driven by consumer demand from one neighboring city to the next. We call it the ripple effect. Even though we were founded in 1907, it wasn't until 1960 we entered the Houston market, approximately seventy-five miles away. In 1964, we went in the opposite direction, entering the Austin area. We took it slow to ensure that we could provide excellent service to those customers that took a chance on us. It was also critical that we consistently maintained the high-quality standards we had established.

In 1989 we ventured across state lines for the first time by opening branches in Oklahoma and Louisiana. The "little creamery" was finally stepping out. This consumer demand expansion philosophy continued throughout the nineties, as we journeyed through Mississippi, Arkansas, Alabama, and Georgia. The only exception to this strategy was when we entered the Kansas City market in 1993. With just a few requests for our products in that area, we decided there were other logistical and supply chain benefits that overrode our normal strategy. To enter a market virtually unknown, surrounded by a sea of competition, meant we had our work cut out for us.

In the summer of 2004, we decided to go rogue and try this strategy again. This time, we looked west for expansion and decided to stealth our way into the blistering hot Arizona market, with Phoenix and Tucson as two new eventual branch locations. This included developing a game plan to go to the market on a moment's notice but without the usual branch facility to support our entrance. Our distribution center (or branch as we refer to it) would be built simultaneously with our opening. To make this work, we operated out of a temporary cold storage facility. This departure from the "consumer demand strategy" was certainly a risk, but one we were willing to take. We believed in our product and our program and felt this opportunity to plant and cultivate a seed (with a lot of patience) would establish a permanent home for many years to come. After getting the green light to go, my next assignment was to purchase land for our future home, and so our journey out west began.

Because Phoenix is such a large city, I knew it would take time to find the best location for our branch. Because our routes run in all directions, being close to a good highway system is always a benefit.

A strong labor base and affordability also play a factor in determining where the distribution facility should be located. Difficult, yes, but I was up for the challenge, even in the Phoenix summer. After a successful first day of property searching, I returned to my hotel with one thing on my mind, "Where's the pool?"

For those of you who know me, swimming isn't high on my list when it comes to recreational activities. However, with the temperature topping 118 that day, it became my number one option. Locals said it was a "dry heat," but it was still 118°. HEAT being the keyword. I quickly changed and was ready to go, or so I thought. The hotel boasted about its variety of swimming pools, ranging from a small kiddie pool area to a large family pool for those of all ages and water activities to the separated adult pool designed for a quieter and more relaxing atmosphere.

Upon entering the pool area, I was immediately greeted by an old childhood memory, THE MONSTER SLIDE. Not just any slide; oh no, no, no. This was a three-story mega slide with twists and turns that would leave the strong begging for more and the weak racing to the kiddie pool. I thought, let's do this. Without hesitation, I made a mad dash to the stairs, double-stepping my way to the launching pad.

As I looked at the water below, my mind filled with flashbacks of rides from the past. I was a kid again, and my heart began to race. Would this live up to my expectations? How fast could I go? Better yet, was the world ready for me to set a new record (in the over-forty division) for the fastest downhill slide? There was only one way to find out.

After the first turn, I knew I was in trouble. I was out of control with no way to slow down, and my initial feeling of excitement was replaced by fear. I began to panic, feeling out of control as I went flying around each corner. How much longer is this ride going to last? Can I make it to the end, or will I shoot across the Arizona sky like a rocket?

As I rounded the last curve, my built-up momentum sent me hydroplaning out of the chute, flipping me upside down and propelling me into the water below. The young lifeguard on duty rushed to my aid, to my mortification. As I quickly tried to regain my composure, he asked if I was alright, to which I replied, "Of course, nothing to see here!" And with that, I asked for directions to the kiddie pool.

Monster Slide – 1

Ricky's Pride – 0

While it's a fun story, and one I take great enjoyment in retelling, this experience still holds a lesson. Because life has a way of doing that to you! One moment you are filled with exciting opportunities and promising expectations, the next moment the world seems upside down and out of control. Fear can do that to you; it can send you spiraling, unable to regain your footing. The answer, though, is to never give up. This is especially true when trying to live a spirit-filled life for Christ. As exciting as it is to live for Christ, the world works overtime to convince you that what they have to offer is better. It's centered around you, and it will come in areas of your life where you are the most vulnerable. Why? That's how the enemy works.

When we encounter struggles, we often look for worldly answers to remedy our situation. The problem is that removing God from the equation also takes the glory away from God and replaces it with earthly deceptions. A great example of this is found in John Chapter 5:

Afterward, Jesus returned to Jerusalem for one of the Jewish holy days. ² Inside the city, near the Sheep Gate, was the pool of Bethesda,[a] with five covered porches. ³ Crowds of sick people—blind, lame, or paralyzed—lay on the porches.[k] *5 One of the men lying there had been sick for thirty-eight years. 6 When Jesus saw him and knew he had been ill for a long time, he asked him, "Would you like to get well?"*

7 "I can't, sir," the sick man said, "for I have no one to put me into the pool when the water bubbles up. Someone else always gets there ahead of me."

8 Jesus told him, "Stand up, pick up your mat, and walk!"

9 Instantly, the man was healed! He rolled up his sleeping mat and began walking!

—JOHN 5: 1–9

For thirty-eight years, this man had laid by the pool waiting for the waters to stir, then trying to be the first in the water to be healed by its magical powers. Thirty-eight years of starting and stopping, only to become so discouraged, he seems to have accepted this way of life.

Sometimes, it's easier to blame our situation than accept our condition, yet in his case, he never gave up hope.

When Jesus saw him, and knowing how long he'd been there, he asked the simple question: "Would you like to get well?" What was an obvious question, seemed to catch him off guard. Instead, he answers with an excuse for why he is still in his current condition. Boy, that sounds familiar. I would rather tell God why I can't than listen to Him on how I can. Excuses can become comfortable and then become a way of life. The problem is, in my weakness, He is made strong.

The key to avoiding this is simple: Suit up and get into the water. Whether your life has become a monster slide adventure or you're just dipping your toes in the kiddie pool, engage in what God has planned for you and leave the reasons "you can't" lying beside the pool of discomfort. Trusting can be awkward and sometimes downright scary, but walking (or swimming) by faith always pleases God more than you can imagine and you will always be rewarded by His blessings.

06

Rental Truck

When I first became acquainted with Blue Bell through my paper at Baylor University, I was struck by their long-term vision and company values. Even though the company had been around since 1907, it remained within itself, not trying to grow too fast, yet growing at a steady pace throughout each season of each year. We determined success by the cinch by the inch mentality, and all who captured this vision embraced it. When many of my fellow classmates were entertained at fancy restaurants located at the top of skyscraper office buildings, I was treated to the local Mr. Gatti's all-you-can-eat pizza parlor in downtown Brenham. There were no country club memberships included in the job offer or fancy company cars to drive. Instead, everyone worked together to get the job done. Each and every day. Titles defined your responsibilities but didn't define your boundaries when it came to helping others when called upon. Office employees would work the production lines, and every manager, from a territory manager to the branch manager, was trained to run a route in the event a driver salesman wasn't able to come to work.

This cinch by the inch philosophy means austerity must be taken seriously by everyone, every day, to make it happen.

One of the best examples of this approach came when we were entering the Houston market for the first time, back in 1960. Blue Bell Supreme ice cream (as it was referred to) was only available around Brenham and surrounding markets. We had made the decision just a few years earlier to discontinue producing butter and devote all our attention to our ice cream products. Taking our packaged ice cream into Houston would be a game changer for our "little creamery," yet the risk and reward meant moving forward instead of stalling or traveling in the opposite direction.

Houston had grown to the seventh largest city in the United States, with people relocating from all over the country. With some persuasive talking of his own, Ed Kruse, our president, was able to convince John Barnhill to come to work for the creamery, join Blue Bell, and head up the Houston sales team. He was excited about the opportunity and immediately began preparing for the numerous sales calls they would have to make with local grocers. As part of any salesman's tools of the trade, he needed a business card to leave at each stop, along with any additional company information and, of course, samples of our ice cream.

When he asked Mr. Kruse about the possibility of procuring his own business cards, Ed gave John a stack of his own cards and told him to cross out what didn't apply. For the record, that was everything on the card except the name of the company.

Looking to save money wherever we could to succeed meant sacrificing *everywhere* possible. This philosophy was instilled throughout the company, and as painful as it might sound, it was the philosophy that laid the foundation for our future.

I have learned over time that it's the difficult challenges that define you, and each and every sacrifice plays a key role when it comes to keeping expenses down. Austerity. This philosophy carried us through the sixties and seventies. And even though we were already seventy-four years old in 1981 when I started, we were still a small regional brand. Each major decision had the potential of opening new doors or closing the book entirely. The Kruses knew the risk but also were totally committed to succeeding with our ice cream in Houston.

Reusing in-house mail envelopes, limiting long-distance phone calls to just the facts, and strategically designing sales routes were just a few of the cost-saving measures we embraced as we expanded. In 1983, In 1983, when I relocated from Fort Worth to San Antonio, the decision was easy. It was an unbelievable opportunity to return to my hometown and introduce Blue Bell to many consumers who had never tried it. Moving also meant selling our house, packing all our belongings, and securing a rental truck for the long move. Sure, having a moving company come in and pack my family's belongings was a normal benefit for most companies, but for Blue Bell, when trying to make every dollar count, the self-move policy was not a problem.

Our entry into San Antonio was an immediate success. Word of mouth had always been our best friend, and our greatest sales tool was the people who were talking about our ice cream! Even though they had only been available in north and central Texas, flavors like Homemade Vanilla and Cookies 'n Cream were embraced by many Texans, and memories began to be crafted around each and every bowl served.

As the company grew and became more successful, more relocations were in my future.

During the company's rapid expansion from 1988 to 1996, I traveled from San Antonio to Oklahoma City to Tulsa to Kansas City and back to Tulsa, then spent 1996 to 2003 overseeing plant operations in Broken Arrow.

Ironically, the new region alignment was created right after I moved into the production side of operations. Little did I know the years running the production plant would eventually prepare me for running the company twenty years later.

But each new opportunity with Blue Bell meant packing and unpacking from one town to the next. Fortunately, our moving policy continued to be modified and eventually included an option to use a moving company. Even so, I still preferred to move myself for reasons today I cannot explain.

Receiving important phone calls had been a pattern throughout my career, but none more important than the one I received in the fall of 2003 from Melvin Ziegenbein, our vice president and general sales manager. He was calling to offer me a way back into sales by assuming part of his duties as general sales manager. Even though this meant returning to Texas, it was a difficult decision to leave Oklahoma. For me, returning to my home state was exciting, but it would be more of a sacrifice for Anita, my wife, moving further from Missouri, where most of her family still lived. I would ask her to make the sacrifice of moving to Texas at the same time we were to become empty nesters. Oklahoma had been our home. It's where we met and where we blended our two families together to include three girls and two boys. Leaving them behind in college and adulthood was by far the toughest part, but we both truly believed that our relocation to Brenham was all part of God's plan.

As excited as I was for the opportunity, I also knew this decision would also require another move. If there was a silver lining to this request, this move would have to be our last. No one had ever been brought to the main office only to return to a branch location, and I

was determined not to be the first. After overseeing our plant operation in Broken Arrow for the past six years, this was an opportunity to
return to the sales department and oversee the marketing and advertising departments as well. I was beyond excited.

Yes, the use of a moving company was by far the "go-to" option from
our family vote, but somehow the self-move packing method came back
into my mind. I eventually convinced my wife it would be fun to move at
our own pace and spread it out over a series of weekends. A decision you
will soon learn would come back to haunt me.

RECALCULATING

The first round of this self-move madness came on Christmas day, 2004.

We had just become empty nesters, and after all the Christmas presents were opened and the family lunch was a distant memory, my wife
and I got in our packed rental truck and headed south. I remember the
day was cloudy, dreary, and cold, with patches of snow bordering both
sides of the highway. The semi-white landscape was there to make it a
Christmas to embrace. We were excited about the move, and as long as
we were together, our plan remained solid.

After a few hours of riding in this luxury rental vehicle, we
decided to stop to stretch our legs and eat dinner. As we pulled into
the next town, we also remembered it was Christmas day and most
places would be closed, so our options would be extremely limited.
Something has to be open … right? After a few failed attempts, the
situation became more concerning. Every Taco Bell, McDonald's,
Jack in the Box, and Burger King was closed, and for good reason.
This was a day to celebrate the birth of our Savior and be with family.
Unless, of course, you decide to travel on this sacred day. The hunger

pangs began to creep in, and starvation in the cold played mind tricks in my head. Surely there has to be something open?

At approximately 7:30 p.m. we entered the town of Atoka, Oklahoma, and were greeted by a well-lit gas station and convenience store. I remember thinking, This is the most beautiful sight there could possibly be. Gas for the truck and potentially the best fried chicken made on that day was such a blessing, and we knew it. With "Chester Chicken" now as my new best friend, Anita and I thought we had hit pay dirt. Semi-clean bathrooms to boot. We refueled, grabbed our chicken, and down the road we went, saved from potential starvation. As we crossed the Red River into Texas, we calculated our time and determined we were almost at the halfway mark.

There was little left of the fried chicken as we acknowledged the "Welcome to Texas" sign and had just started to make our way through the assortment of packaged cookies and pork rinds when a terrible sound came from the front-right side of the truck. The highway was dark, and we were right in the middle of a construction zone with cement bumper pads on both sides of the road, boxing us in with nowhere to pull over. Anita saw smoke coming from the front of the truck, and the earlier prayers for food were immediately replaced with prayers for help and safety. "Jesus Take the Wheel" had yet to be written, but we needed Him to take charge and in a hurry.

And, faithfully, He did. God brought us through to the other side of the construction madness, and I was able to make it over to the shoulder of the road, out of harm's way. It was as dark of a night as it could be, with just the lights from the passing cars to assist us in determining the damage. Anita opened her side of the truck, stepped out, and immediately discovered the problem at hand. She turned to me, "The wheel has come off the truck!" "The tire—don't you mean the tire?" I asked. As soon as the words left my mouth, I realized by her expression that her knowledge of trucks trumped my disbelief in her response. In a calm but direct voice, she repeated the same phrase, this time with about a dozen exclamation marks after the word wheel. "Yes, the wheel is sideways and serving as a kickstand, keeping us from rolling down the hill." At that, I decided it might be good to get out of the truck as well. Navigating the oncoming traffic, I was able to make it safely to the other side and saw firsthand what she had perfectly described.

Using the flashlight on my phone, I pulled myself up over the tire and confirmed what others already knew—that my wife was a lot smarter than I had given her credit for. Sure enough, our luxurious twenty-six-foot rental limousine was down for the count. We were stranded. Did I mention it was Christmas night, and there was snow on the ground?

We called the rental company to explain our circumstances. I was frustrated but still managed to maintain a relatively calm demeanor. I knew I had rolled the dice, and instead of hitting the jackpot, I had put us in harm's way. After a series of automated menu options on my cell phone, pressing three connected me to roadside service. The greatest feeling in the world came over me, one you've probably experienced, when a live human's voice finally answered the call.

As she asked questions to assess the situation and our location, I proceeded to tell her that the wheel had snapped off the tie-rod and was hanging on only by the brake fluid line. Her response was pretty similar to mine, "Oh, you need a tire." I quickly answered that, no, I need a new tie-rod. The tire was still on the wheel and in good shape.

Now, I'm not the most mechanically inclined person in the world, but my response bounced off the backboard and fell onto deaf ears. She proceeded to repeat her assessment, asking the size of tire I would need to replace the flat. Again, but with a little more charismatic Christian love, I told her the tire was fine, it was the wheel and tie-rod that needed repair.

For most, this second attempt would clear up the confusion, but for the lady that happened to draw the Christmas night hotline duty, truck repairs were way beyond her pay grade. So, we moved on to the next question.

She said she wanted to help us as quickly as possible, but she first needed my location, which was approximately five miles south of the Texas-Oklahoma border on Hwy 75. I was taught early in my driving days to keep up with the road markers as I traveled in the event I broke down, but with all the excitement of the wheel coming off, I couldn't determine my exact landmark. She again asked me about my specific location, to which I tried to give her all the information I could.

I'm not sure if it was the tone of her voice or just the level of frustration that had taken over my emotions, but when she asked me, "Are you sure you're in Texas?" it took all I had to keep my thoughts in check. After a few more unrelated questions, she put me on hold and finally returned with a game plan. A tow truck was on the way and would get us to the next town where we would stay for the night. During our wait, we walked down the embankment, then climbed up to the entrance to a prefabbed home sales lot where we found a bench to sit on under a single security light.

As we waited for the truck to arrive, Anita began warming her hands while I replayed our events of the evening over and over, wondering how I had gotten us into this mess. But despite our frustration, it turned to thankfulness and praise to God, realizing how this night could have turned out much differently.

In those moments, looking out in the night sky, our focus returned to what day it was—Christmas. No matter how bad things seemed, it was nothing compared to the night Mary and Joseph traveled to Bethlehem. They had no comfortable truck to ride in or freshly made fried chicken to eat. No phone to call for help or even call ahead for reservations. No tow truck to take them to a hotel where they would either get a good night's sleep or, even more importantly, bring our Lord and Savior into the world. Who were we to complain about our situation compared to the entrance of our Savior, whose first night on Earth meant sleeping in a stable, shared by farm animals and their offensive fragrance.

Our predicament is often created by our own choices—choices we make minutes, hours, or days prior to *the predicament*. It starts with choice. Thinking back in time, it was just one forbidden fruit that birthed choice. Curiosity will do that to you when you're not prepared to stand strong. From that one bad choice came a series of bad choices—too many to count—and they continue to multiply over and over to this very day. With knowledge came self-centeredness, and it sent our daily focus inward instead of upward. We want to follow the path which God has laid out for each of our lives, yet we want to do it on our terms. We want to make our own choices, forcing God to constantly say "recalculating."

The ability to "choose," from Adam and Eve all the way to you and me, is the author of history. Each choice that we make determines a path of events that keeps this world turning. It begins the moment one is born, and instinctively, even as a newborn, we want to choose. We will choose when to eat, where to go, and what to do with our independence and every other decision until the day we die. This human nature gift, as wonderful as it might sound, has doomed us from the start. With one exception: The freedom to choose Christ!

From the garden to the birth of the Son of man, history has continued to repeat itself, and this strategic independent "choice" has failed miserably. Praise God that Jesus came into the world at just the right time to pay the price for those who put their faith in Him. But the empty tomb also stared death in the face and said ... Not today! In fact, not for eternity!

Yes, Jesus came into the world "to save sinners," as we read in 1 Timothy 1:15:

This is a trustworthy saying, and everyone should accept it: "Christ Jesus came into the world to save sinners"—and I am the worst of them all.

But he also came to destroy the enemy:

But when people keep on sinning, it shows that they belong to the devil, who has been sinning since the beginning. But the Son of God came to destroy the works of the devil.

—1 JOHN 3:8

Whether the devil made me do it or my fleshly human desires constantly trying to take control, it's only when I die to self, daily, that I release the power of choice from my hands and lay it at the feet of the cross. Is it a struggle? Yes! Do I fail on a regular basis? Yes! But thanks to God's love and grace, He is there to pick up the pieces and get me back on the right track.

After a long and eventful day, we remembered that this was His day. Two thousand years ago, He left the throne and came into a broken world to eventually pay the ultimate price. Within a couple of hours, the wrecker service showed up on the scene and was able to get us to the hotel in the next city. Unlike our Lord and Savior, the hotel had a room waiting for us, and for that, we were ever so grateful.

07

Crisis

When my cell phone rang at 6:45 p.m. on that Friday evening back in 2015, the caller ID displayed our president and CEO at Blue Bell. To be getting a call on a Friday night indicated that something was out of the ordinary at best. Good news was generally saved for Monday, so even before I answered, my imagination was in overdrive. In those initial few seconds, my thoughts went from the possibility that his dad, Ed Kruse, and leader of our company for so many years, had fallen ill to there being something wrong at the plant.

Uncertainty of the unknown can cause immediate anxiety, which tends to lead to fear. Emotions like this can have a way of taking over when you are least prepared, and nothing had prepared me for what was next. As my anxiousness reached the pit of my stomach, I began to draw a variety of other conclusions, none of which were good. And with that, I answered the call. Unfortunately, my intuition was right. The Texas Department of Health Services had just notified our company that certain Blue Bell frozen snacks had tested positive for *Listeria monocytogenes*. We were shocked, and our hearts were broken by this news.

According to the Food and Drug Agency, *Listeria monocytogenes,* also known as *L. mono*, is a species of pathogenic (disease-causing) bacteria that can be found in moist environments, soil, water, decaying vegetation, and animals, and can survive and even grow under refrigeration and other food preservation measures. The FDA states that listeria can cause a range of symptoms from fever and muscle aches to potentially becoming fatal, especially among the elderly and those that have a weakened immune system. Listeria can also be dangerous for pregnant women and their newborn babies.

Listeria identification in any frozen, ready-to-eat product is rare, especially in ice cream, where the product is pasteurized and then frozen before it even reaches the carton. Regardless of this low-risk potential, we knew we needed to react immediately. As concerning as the news was, we were confident we could get ahead of it and would work diligently to isolate and eliminate *L. mono* from our products and environment.

In the days and weeks that followed, unfortunately, the situation seemed to only escalate as new test results identified *L. mono* in other parts of our plant in Brenham, as well as in our second manufacturing plant, located in Broken Arrow, Oklahoma. As critical as the situation had become, nothing prepared us for the devastating news that the Center for Disease Control had matched our listeria DNA with three deaths and ten illnesses through a process called whole genome sequencing. Similar to a fingerprint, this process determines the complete DNA sequence of an organism's genome. This news was truly heartbreaking and drove us to our knees.

What we learned over the next few months changed the course of how we were to attack this unknown enemy. A true seek and destroy mission was in full operation, yet time was not on our side.

With the situation reaching a critical point, on April 20, 2015, I sat in the room and weighed in on the decision to shut down all three manufacturing plants and issue a nationwide recall on all products produced by Blue Bell. This included every pint, half gallon, three gallons, take-home and bulk frozen snacks. Within the next few weeks, over eight million gallons of ice cream products were returned and destroyed from all accounts throughout the country, and the total inventory was also destroyed at all Blue Bell facilities. Doing the right thing didn't come without consequences: We shut down all plant and branch facilities, furloughed longtime employees, and laid off employees for the first time in the history of the company. It was crushing to have to explain this to those affected by this decision, but we truly believed that if we took the proper steps to eliminate listeria, we would be able to reopen soon.

When dealing with listeria, it's critical to locate its source of entry, then go to extreme measures to follow its path all the way to the product. It's also essential to develop a plan to keep this situation from happening again. With the assistance of a top microbiologist, this commitment was embraced by employees throughout the company and our culture of excellence went into overdrive. Even though we were confident in the quality standards that were in place, we knew we had the responsibility of taking our procedures to a new level. This included a high level of transparency, staying humble and honest, and staying relentless to this commitment. For the days and months that followed, we worked around the clock to make the necessary changes to achieve this goal, and these changes were monumental. We took a top-to-bottom approach looking at our facilities, policies, and procedures. All were reviewed and enhancements were made. Floors, ceilings, and production walls were replaced. Employee standard operating procedures were enhanced, and entry into and exit from the plant were limited, just to name a few of the measures taken. The daunting task of this unfamiliar challenge also drove us to our knees, causing us to be totally dependent on God's grace and direction. Looking for peace in the middle of a storm meant looking up instead of looking in and then trusting.

> **"Looking for peace in the middle of a storm meant looking up instead of looking in, and then trusting."**

Fear can rapidly set up shop at times like this and must be tackled head-on before it takes root. Fear also tends to zero in on worst-case scenarios when evaluating potential outcomes. It's here where you have to choose which direction to run—away from God's direction or into the arms of God's direction and grace. From experience, I have found that choosing to run away only delays the inevitable.

When you finally get to a place where you can totally let go and allow God to turn your fears into faith, He will provide a peace that surpasses all understanding. This assurance comes from a God who loves you more than you can ever comprehend, and He is there to guide you every step of the way. It's the faith of a child when things don't make sense. It's the kind of faith that gave Shadrach, Meshach, and Abednego the confidence to walk into the furnace, trusting God, no matter the outcome. It's the kind of faith Daniel had as he was lowered into the den of lions. It's the kind of faith that can give you permanent residency in Heaven for all eternity, when placing your trust in God's Son as your Savior.

It's not the amount of faith you have; it's where you place it! I have learned that when things don't make sense, get as close to God as you can. Leave fear at the door and walk with an unexplainable faith.

Because we live in a broken world, there will be a point when each of us will be faced with *unbearable* circumstances: The troubling news from a doctor concerning one's health, a marriage that has been destroyed by adultery, or the loss of a loved one, to name just a few. Such news will take you places no one wants to go and most always is accompanied by the unwelcome emotion of fear. It's a natural place for your mind to run, and normally, in a crisis, fearing the worst takes center stage instead of seeking peace in the middle of the trial. Again, in most situations, it's the fear of the potential outcome that sends our minds into overdrive.

When analyzing this thing called fear, two main characteristics come to mind. Funnily enough, they take us in opposite directions. The first is fear of a "potential outcome," and it is typically the worst. The second is the "fear of reverence" or being enamored by someone or something. Think of it as coming into the presence of a celebrity or someone you highly admire, or possibly during those early teenage years when you see that cute girl for the first time. Getting the courage to just say hello can be accompanied by a bad case of sweaty palms, tongue-tying dialogue, and a heavy dose of "lack of self-confidence."

Talk about fear! I remember seeing my wife for the first time. It was at our church's singles night at a minor league hockey game. After spotting her, I remember that high level of "excitement fear" that took over and the wishful and promising thought of, "So you say there's a chance for us?" After twenty-six years of marriage, there is still the element of fear involved, but that's for a different book.

For me, the best example of this overwhelming, overpowering, and enamoring experience is when I come before the presence of our Lord. There are so many passages in scripture that teach about the "fear of the

Lord," yet because of our unworthiness, we tend to run away from God instead of running towards Him. When I have stripped away my pride, my self-centeredness, and all things that separate me from God, I find a peace in His presence that seems to come with a heart of brokenness.

With brokenness, my desperation brings me back around to fear, only this time fear would be in reverence and dependency of God Almighty. I truly believe, the fear of the Lord is the starting line of this thing called "life" and replaces the fear of uncertainty when total trust is placed in Him in everything you say and do. Proverbs 9:10 describes it beautifully:

The fear of the Lord is the beginning of wisdom, and the knowledge of the Holy One is insight.

And even more pointed verses are found in Philippians 4:6–7:

Do not be anxious about anything, but in every situation, by prayer and petition, with thanksgiving, present your requests to God. And the peace of God, which transcends all understanding, will guard your hearts and your minds in Christ Jesus.

So how can we break free from this bondage called fear and rest in this incredible "peace-like faith," no matter the circumstances or eventual outcome?

We need to start at the very beginning, in the book of Genesis, where we find Adam and Eve walking in the garden of Eden.

I can't imagine what life must have been like. Beautiful surroundings, unlimited amounts of every kind of fruit and vegetable at their disposal (with the exception of one), and the ability to truly walk with God, independent of any possible distractions—or *so they thought!*

For Adam and Eve, the only element of fear that existed was reverence for God Almighty. The ability to walk and talk with the creator of the universe had to be indescribable, each day filled with loving each other and praising God. One thing was certain: Life was good.

It wasn't until spiritual warfare slid into the garden in the form of a snake and pricked their curiosity that the other kind of "fear" entered the world. At this point, they probably only had a sense of curiosity, but fear was not present. Unfortunately, this curiosity got the best of them, and the next thing they knew, they were heading straight to the forbidden fruit. This lack of fear is evident when neither Adam nor Eve are bothered by a talking snake. I'm not sure about you but talking to a snake would be the last thing I would want to do. Even though life was good, after just one bite, the world as they knew it changed!

Oh, and to be so close to the Tree of Life (everlasting life) and yet fall for the temptation of the desire of knowledge definitely had a direct and sinful effect on all of mankind from that point all the way to eternity. I have always wondered what life would have been like if either of them had first eaten from the Tree of Life. Everlasting life instead of pain and suffering? Maybe something to look forward to in Heaven!

From the moment Adam and Eve obtained this knowledge, they learned about this thing called "good and evil" and the consequences that followed their actions. They also may have realized they had just become the original cast for *Naked and Afraid.* It was one thing to be totally exposed through their nakedness with each other, but things got increasingly worse when God entered the garden.

We read in Genesis 3:10:

8 When the cool evening breezes were blowing, the man[a] and his wife heard the LORD God walking about in the garden. So, they hid from the LORD *God among the trees.* *⁹ Then the* LORD *God called to the man, "Where are you?"*

¹⁰ He replied, "I heard you walking in the garden, so I hid. I was afraid because I was naked."

Afraid and all alone, when you are caught in the middle of a place you never intended to go, can leave you feeling isolated and helpless. I can only imagine the overwhelming feeling of these new emotions called *fear* and *shame* that instinctively led them to hide when they heard God approaching. Because their eyes were open to knowledge, they also felt exposed physically and rushed to make clothes to cover themselves. The result of their decision changed the trajectory of all of mankind, and with their newfound knowledge came evil and, eventually, death. Also, with this newfound gift of knowledge came the renewed gift of choice, and it has been handed down from generation to generation.

We love the ability to make decisions, but with each decision, there is an outcome, and the journey continues. These decisions include who to date, where to live, or where to work, to name just a few. From those initial decisions, more decisions and consequences will follow until we one day finish the race.

Although what happened to our company in 2015 wasn't premeditated, the consequences led to our unfortunate circumstances. No one or no company is immune to a potential crisis; therefore, it's critical that with every decision, there is a risk study of the potential outcome.

Our aggressive new plan included a robust environmental testing program to identify the enemy in the event it was to make its way through the door. We also began testing every batch, on every production line, at every plant, every day! We refer to this process as our "hold and test" program, which gives additional assurance that every product produced is safe. We have also invited additional outside agencies to inspect all of our facilities and review these procedures for additional certification.

You know what, sin is a lot like this harmful *Listeria monocytogenes* pathogen. Like *L. mono*, sin is all around every one of us, at all times, every day, lurking in the shadows and waiting for the proper moment to be invited in. Even if it's unintentional. Just ask Adam and Eve! Once sin sets up shop, the process begins, and unless it's identified and dealt with, it will run rapidly and eventually destroy. Sin, in its truest form, means separation from God and turns you from a dependency on God to total isolation. Praise God there is a thing called forgiveness through repentance, but this human example of "test and hold" requires you to turn and go the opposite direction, once sin is identified.

No matter the circumstance you find yourself in, finding peace in any storm comes when one lets go and allows God to take the steering wheel. Trust comes at the most crucial times in our lives, but faith is all that is required to enter His presence. People still talk about what happened to the "little creamery" in 2015, yet almost ten years later, I can tell you it was by God's grace we were able to make it to the other side.

08

Hurricane Season

There is not a better time of the year than summer—especially if you're in the ice cream business. For Blue Bell, the summer months are the most exciting of all the seasons, yet they can be the most intense and challenging. Ice cream production normally runs at full capacity, and our sales team works diligently across the country to stock the shelves of every grocer with (hopefully) every customer's favorite flavors. No doubt, the summer keeps us going strong. We deliver all our products straight to each account by using our own route trucks and trained sales personnel. This preferred system is better known as direct store delivery or DSD. Because ice cream is such a fragile product, going this extra step and eliminating going through a warehouse protects each half gallon, pint, and frozen snack from the ever-changing environmental temperatures.

Similar to the downbeat given by an orchestra conductor, the start of this crazy time begins with the sounds of the final school bells ringing all across the country. Even though summer doesn't officially start until June 21st, the end of the school year means the start of numerous trips to local swimming pools, eating plenty of ice cream (of course!), and possibly taking that long-awaited summer family vacation, where memories are sure to be made. Along with the highly anticipated release of summer fun comes the predictable summer heat. It's also when the unpredictable threat of hurricanes occurs, with its season starting on June 1ˢᵗ and running until the end of November.

Hurricanes can develop rapidly when the conditions are right and can be one of the most dangerous acts of mother nature our planet can produce. Each hurricane has its own personality and attitude and can be as predictable as trying to select the weekly winning Power Ball numbers (for those who like to pay to dream big). Unfortunately, neither produces good results. The summer of 2005 was no different. As exciting as the summer season appeared to be, the stage was set for a roller coaster ride of potential storms.

This projection was created by a rare type of El Niño climate pattern that had lingered from 2004. By the end of that year, there were a total of nine hurricanes, six classified as major. As powerful as hurricanes in 2004 turned out to be, 2005 hurricanes looked back and said, "Hold my ice cream cone." The 2005 season went on record as the second most active in recorded history, and by the end of the year, there was a record high of fifteen hurricanes, seven exceeding the category 3 level. Emily, Katrina, Rita, and Wilma, all reaching category 5 status.

Because of this annual threat, our branch locations are on alert for any weather developments that might occur. With over sixty-six branches throughout the southwest, south-central, and southeast markets, many are located in cities from south Texas, all across the coastline of the Gulf of Mexico and up the eastern coastline. To say we are in the eye of any potential storm at any given time would put it lightly.

Up until 2005, we were fortunate to have avoided any significant damage from these powerful storms. But each storm created an acute awareness of its power and prompted us to always prepare for the worst, yet pray for the best. God never promised He would take you out of the storm, but He did promise He'd lead you through it and never leave you alone. We believed in this promise and would soon be put to the test.

On August 19th, the tenth tropical depression of the season developed in the Atlantic waters east of the Bahamas. Like any tropical depression, it got our attention—all related branches were put on alert. On the morning of Wednesday, August 24th, tropical depression 12 strengthened into a tropical storm and was given the name Katrina. A name that will be remembered for many years to come.

On the morning of August 25th, and within hours of making landfall in southern Florida, Tropical Storm Katrina became Hurricane Katrina. By this point, our branches in Miami, Punta Gorda, Orlando, and Tampa had been locked down, bracing for what was coming their way.

Throughout the day, Katrina pushed her way across southern Florida, leaving a path of destruction as her calling card. Even though the dry land tried to slow her down, she had other plans once she crossed back into the warm waters of the Gulf of Mexico on Friday, August 26th. Like a prize fighter who refused to quit, Katrina began to strengthen again and also began shifting toward the Alabama-Mississippi border.

With the threat of any hurricane, there is always the potential risk of personal injury, great property damage, and even loss of life. Because of this, our branch follows a strict operational procedure to ensure employee safety. With the potential strength of Katrina, and in accordance with our branch shutdown in southern Florida, we began discontinuing service to all stores and preparing the branches for closure. This also allowed employees ample time to return to their families and seek shelter on higher ground. On Friday afternoon, with Katrina in the Gulf of Mexico, our branches located in New Orleans, Lake Charles, and Mobile had been closed, and everyone was sent home. There was a storm coming, and with the uncertainty of where it would make landfall, we had to be prepared.

On Saturday, August 27th, Katrina reached Category 3, becoming the third major storm of the season. At 10:00 a.m. that day, with Katrina moving through the center of the Gulf of Mexico, the National Hurricane Center issued a Hurricane Watch all the way from Morgan City, Louisiana, to the Louisiana/Mississippi border, including New Orleans. By 6:00 a.m. Sunday morning, Hurricane Katrina became a Category 5 hurricane, with sustained winds of 175 mph. She had set her sights on Louisiana, and it became apparent that this was going to be a terrible storm to reckon with. Throughout the day, she moved closer and closer to the Louisiana coast with wind gusts over 190 mph.

It was during the early morning hours on Monday, August 30th, that Katrina made landfall, and her destructive path took her up through Louisiana, Tennessee, and then on in a northeasterly path.

This powerful storm caused fifty-three breaches of flood protection, including levees designed to protect New Orleans from flooding. Unfortunately, over 80 percent of the city was submerged. Additionally, the hurricane had affected approximately fifteen million people, impacting over ninety thousand square miles of territory from central Florida to eastern Texas. Thirty-three tornados were reported, and the storm surge reached thirty feet.

Once the storm moved through the area, our team began calling to check on employees that had fled to northern Louisiana, Texas, and Arkansas to confirm their safety, an extremely difficult task with cell service almost nonexistent. After a few days of checking, everyone was accounted for and, thankfully, had gotten out of harm's way. To our amazement, none of our employees had any significant damage to their homes.

As for our branch location in Slidell, Louisiana, the initial news was not so promising. All reports that we received indicated that our branch was underwater. It was obviously not the news we were hoping for, but knowing everyone was safe was all that mattered. On the morning of Tuesday, August 29th, our branch manager, Ron Davis, decided to try and get into the branch to confirm our worst fears. To his surprise, he found just the opposite. Visible damage was done to each of the buildings located on each side of our branch, but there was very little damage to our branch itself. Great news!

His next report indicated that a large tree had fallen onto our property and landed where our bobtail trucks were parked. At first, it was thought that at least one truck was damaged, along with minor damage to our outer fence. Upon further inspection, it was discovered that where the tree had fallen, there was only vacant space. The truck that was normally parked in that spot was in the shop for service, leaving an empty space for this unwanted visitor.

More great news!

The next question was, "Was the shop underwater?" Our concern was soon confirmed. Everything in the area had been flooded, and everything was underwater. Not good news! While we counted our blessing that no one was hurt and there was limited damage, word came in that even though the shop was under a few feet of water, the truck itself had been raised up on the lift to be serviced and left there when the building was evacuated. The lift had kept the truck from the flood waters below. More great news!

In the days and weeks ahead, we were able to remove all of our ice cream products from our cold storage facility, then convert the branch into a command center for emergency service and first responders. Using a generator as our power source and cold storage as a freezer, food was brought in by the pallet loads for all the sheriff's departments and first responders on the scene.

Even though the good-news-bad-news-good-news sequence of events ended well for us, we were all devastated by the destruction and for the people who lost their lives in the powerful storm.

There were also tens of thousands who were left homeless, with all their possessions destroyed except for what they could take with them as they evacuated.

Storms can develop at any time in our life, and inevitably, they always seem to come when we least expect them. Unlike hurricanes, though, there is no predictable season to prepare for nor can we always forecast a model to give us any warning.

And with each storm, there comes the natural question of … Why?

It's in those moments that—through a lack of understanding—fear turns to anger and drives us to this simple yet demanding question: Why? I have found the answer in the deafening silence: trust.

I don't have to like it, but how I handle my circumstances will define who I am. Realizing I live in a broken world and knowing storms can overpower my faith, I resort to praying the hardest four words of any prayer, "Thy will be done," especially when praying to God through a difficult time. It's only when you let go and let God take control, no matter how difficult, that you will find peace that calms the waters.

Asking "why" is a fair and honest question, yet many times, the answer is to wait. When this happens, fear tries to move in. I have found that when things don't seem to make sense, I have the choice to either run to God or run from Him, and my reaction is based on how afraid I am of what His answer might be. It's also the time I need to be reminded that He is still in control and loves me in a way I will never comprehend. On the other hand, running from God only compounds the situation and has the tendency to turn fear into anger.

A great illustration of this process comes from the movie *Forrest Gump* when Forrest and Lieutenant Dan get caught in a terrible storm during a shrimp expedition. Lieutenant Dan was already bitter and angry at God for not allowing him to die on the battlefield like some of his family members before him, instead leaving him permanently disabled. Even though it seems through this scene that Lieutenant Dan is downright sacrilegious, it shows he's able to uncork his bottled-up emotions and anger toward God by drawing close to Him, instead of running from Him. As the sun comes up and Dan looks around, he realizes his boat was the only boat spared from the storm as they make their way back to shore. It's at that moment his emotions turn from anger to joy! From blame to acceptance, from fear to faith, he makes peace with his circumstances and with God.

This is not an easy process, and again, when difficult situations don't make sense, remember the storm didn't take God by surprise, and the outcome won't either, even if you don't understand it until you reach Heaven. Trust and peace are the hardest emotions to grab hold of, especially when it's dark. But remember: In every situation, grace will begin to take root when you trade fear for trust.

One final example of this is found in Mark 4: 35–41:

> ^{35} *That day, when evening came, he said to his disciples, "Let us go over to the other side." ^{36} Leaving the crowd behind, they took him along, just as he was, in the boat. There were also other boats with him. ^{37} A furious squall came up, and the waves broke over the boat so that it was nearly swamped. ^{38} Jesus was in the stern, sleeping on a cushion. The disciples woke him and said to him, "Teacher, don't you care if we drown?"*
>
> ^{39} *He got up, rebuked the wind, and said to the waves, "Quiet! Be still!" Then, the wind died down, and it was completely calm.*
>
> ^{40} *He said to his disciples, "Why are you so afraid? Do you still have no faith?"*

⁴¹ They were terrified and asked each other, "Who is this? Even the wind and the waves obey him!"

Jesus knew the storm was coming, yet He knew who was in control. When all the others panicked, He slept. When things seemed to be out of control, He continued to sleep. In the darkest moments of the storm, and as the boat begins taking on water, they run out of options and run to the Savior. How could Jesus sleep during such a storm? Could He not have gotten up and calmed the storm before the disciples reached the point of total desperation? Fortunately, He slept until they approached Him. It was the storm that drove them to Him and, in this case, His power over the seas that made them ask, "Who is this? Even the wind and the waves obey him!"

After rebuking the storm, He reminds them not to be afraid. Yes, in life, there will be storms—guaranteed. And when the storms turn into hurricanes, go to the front of the boat, if you're not already there, and lay at the feet of Jesus and rest. Continually pray for peace when the waves come over you and for power when fear and doubt set in.

For me, one of the most powerful storms that came into my life was when, in 1996, I realized my first marriage was over. In the darkest hours of desperation, I cried out to God, looking for answers, not understanding how our foundation had shifted. It was in those moments that God reminded me that the gift of choice comes with consequences, and just like a broken world, our marriage was broken by choices. It was also during this time that this passage came alive in my life. For the days, weeks, and months that followed, I gravitated to this passage, curled up next to Jesus, and found rest in His love. I found the peace that surpasses all understanding and strength to face the next day.

The days that followed also meant keeping my children grounded.

Through faithfulness, God blessed me beyond measure by placing Anita in my life. Blending a family of five (my three kids and her two) came with challenges of its own, but through the grace of God, we made it through. Today, we have been married for over twenty-six years and enjoy eight grandkids as well as their parents. What has gotten us through each challenge was that our faith was centered on Christ. Have there been storms in those years? Absolutely, but we continue to run to the front of the boat, hold on tight, and trust that Christ will once again guide us through.

Psalm 107: 28–30 reads:

> [28] *Then they cried out to the Lord in their trouble,*
>   *and he brought them out of their distress.*
> [29] *He stilled the storm to a whisper;*
>   *the waves of the sea[a] were hushed.*
> [30] *They were glad when it grew calm,*
>   *and he guided them to their desired haven.*

The days, weeks, and months that followed the devastating destruction of Hurricane Katrina left many with questions that had no answers. Even though we had made it through the storm, our hearts still went out to those who weren't so fortunate. Lives were lost. Homes and businesses were destroyed. Families pulled apart or displaced. Storms have a way of doing that.

I have come to believe that when things don't add up, get ready, because God is still on the throne, and He is working. I also am reminded that the scars are on the hands and side of His Son. A price for the sinful brokenness that covers this world, yet by His grace, through trusting in Him, there can be peace in the heart of the storm … even when they come unexpectedly and turn into hurricanes.

09

What to Wear

In August 2007, the Brenham Creamery Company, better known today as Blue Bell Creameries, turned one hundred years old. To say this was an amazing accomplishment would be an understatement. Normally, turning one hundred means you're close to reaching the end, but most of us at Blue Bell felt like we were just getting started. The impressive list of other companies that had joined this century club included the likes of Coca-Cola, UPS, Boeing, Harley-Davidson, and Dr Pepper, just to name a few. For the limited number of companies that have endured this test of time, there are many others that came up short.

As gratifying as it is to make and sell ice cream, the entire process really comes down to making memories. A certain flavor can take you back to a special place in life that you might have shared with a loved one, or it possibly helped erase a bad day. Ice cream can do that, if it's made right.

To capture the heart of our company, there's nothing more rewarding than engaging with our employees. They are the heart and soul of who we are. I absolutely love walking the production floor or visiting one of our branch sites and catching the dedication from our employees that makes this magic happen. The enthusiasm from all parts of our selling area is contagious. I'll never forget the time in our plant in Brenham when I asked one of our production operators how he was doing, and he yelled out, "I'm living the dream, making the cream." That's what it's all about.

"I'm living the dream, making the cream." That's what it's all about.

In preparation for the 100th anniversary, our company decided to celebrate this major accomplishment in three separate phases. For the first, we had an employee and family celebration cookout, including games and entertainment. Second, we planned a city-wide celebration, where those that came could sample over forty-eight different flavors of ice cream at no charge.

For the third and final event, we hosted a special appreciation dinner for our shareholders, followed by a customer appreciation dinner the next evening. You only turn one hundred once, and we wanted to do it right.

The goal of the event was to make each night as memorable as possible. With estimated crowds of more than one thousand people each night, the logistics were complicated, but with two years of planning, we felt we could make it magical. It started with having a specially designed large tent brought in and constructed on our employee parking lot, which was then transformed into a beautiful banquet hall. Inside the tent, 125 tables of eight were placed around a large circular stage that was positioned in the middle of the room.

Because of the size of the room, large monitors were built that would rival AT&T stadium and were positioned to allow every seat in the house the opportunity to watch the program in comfort. A special outdoor kitchen was built just outside the tent to provide a masterful dinner, rivaling any 5-star restaurant.

Along with special guest speakers and music, we also extended an invitation to President George and Barbara Bush. Now, I have to pause here and explain that Ed and Howard Kruse had been longtime friends of the Bushes and, along with also being Texas A&M fans, the Bushes enjoyed Blue Bell ice cream whenever they were home in Houston.

Unfortunately, they were not able to attend, but they sent a video congratulating the Kruse family and Blue Bell employees on their accomplishment.

The first night went off without a hitch. The weather was spectacular, and the specially prepared dinner was cooked to perfection. After the meal, a special program took the crowd down memory lane, recapping the highs and lows of the past one hundred years. It truly was a wonderful night.

On the second night, we weren't so lucky. Just about the time everyone began to arrive, the skies opened. Over the next few hours, rain comparable to that in Noah's day came in waves. All in all, we received up to six inches of rain. We actually considered pairing up half gallon flavors two by two, just in case. Having a thousand people in a tent during a major storm isn't the most ideal way to celebrate, but with multiple wet-vacs and an understanding crowd, the dinner and program went off without any other major complications.

As successful as the celebrations turned out to be, the planning sessions that took place the two years prior meant many hours away from home. Because of this, I promised my wife, Anita, I would take her on a vacation of her choice when it was over. We'd travel somewhere far away from Brenham to recover from all the activities. A supportive spouse made things easier, and this trip was long overdue and much-needed for both of us.

While trying to make the decision, I remembered her bucket list included a trip to Maine with as many lighthouses and fishing opportunities as possible.

I obviously married well for having a wife who loves to fish, but therein lies the problem. She's good at it, and nine times out of ten, she'll out fish me. And yes, she baits her own hook and reels in her own fish, all while I'm trying to just get a hook in the water. I am okay with fishing, but when I go, I have to check my ego at the dock, then set my iPhone to camera, and get ready for another embarrassing day on the water. Salt water, fresh water, lake, sea, or stream—it always leads to the same results. She's good, and the pictures on my camera back it up. Fishing is great, but it falls to a distant second to seeing lighthouses when given the option. Maybe in Maine my luck would turn around?

With the Texas heat reaching its peak in August, I thought the trip sounded like a great idea—even the fishing. If she's happy, then I'm happy. So, plans were made, and we were all set to begin this adventure the week after the celebration dinners. This trip included a trip to Kennebunkport, Portland, and Camden, Maine.

Three weeks before the event, my wife called and said she had been thinking. "Since we were going to Kennebunkport, we ought to reach out to the Bush family and see if we could bring them some ice cream. Because the Bushes weren't able to make the celebration, maybe we could take a small token of our appreciation to them." My first thought was ... *Right, like they would want to see us*, or better yet, *How do I get the number of a retired President of the United States?* Would they really want us to bring ice cream? Most importantly, in the event they said yes, how in the world would we get it to them since Blue Bell was not available in Maine?

Crazy yes, but it was worth the try, so off I went to work on the details.

Because the Bushes had ordered Blue Bell in the past, I was fortunate to obtain a contact for them. Step one was now in play, and a call was placed with this most unusual request. Approximately one week later, to my surprise, I received a return call from one of the presidential aides requesting that Anita and I come and visit—bringing ice cream, of course. It was also at that moment that, in some cases, working for Blue Bell opened doors that very few other products would be able to do. Especially Mint Chocolate Chip and Coffee ice cream, two of Barbara's favorites.

When the time came to pack for this amazing adventure, I remember standing in my closet, perplexed about what to wear for this once-in-a-lifetime experience. I yelled out to my wife and asked, "What do you wear when you meet the President?" I mean, a suit would be over the top. Yet, jeans and a dress shirt just didn't feel right either. As all good wives do, she yelled back, "It's not about what you wear, it's about you being you." I imagine anyone reading this would probably think the same thing I did: "O.K., that didn't help much." (This is because I'm known for wearing neckties most of the time.) But thinking for a minute, I realized the message she was sending: Look nice, but don't overthink.

To be at the Bushes at the requested time, we had to rearrange our flight schedule and arrive the night before in New Hampshire. This would also eliminate any possible flight delays or cancellations and give us plenty of time to arrive with our special cargo. We had two separate Styrofoam ice chests loaded with ice cream and dry ice and had them sent on ahead. One was sent to the hotel we would be staying in the night before, and the second was sent to our bed and breakfast accommodations in Kennebunkport. This way, if one cooler didn't make it, we would have a backup plan waiting for us the next morning. Luckily, both ice chests made it, and the ice cream was still in great shape.

We woke up early the next morning and prepared for the short trip to Kennebunkport. Our first stop was to swing by the bed and breakfast location and pick up the second ice chest. The manager of the B&B seemed puzzled because the delivery driver had commented that he had a few more orders of Blue Bell to be delivered to the Bushes later that morning. I was unaware of any other order, and I began to wonder who else was using the Blue Bell calling card to visit the President. Come to find out, they had a family reunion the next day.

We grabbed our precious cargo, and off we went. Maybe we could get there before the other shipment arrived? I guess because of the excitement and my OCD tendencies, we ended up arriving about an hour earlier than our appointed time. The good news was we made it!

To kill some time, we parked in an area across from the compound that looked over what is referred to as Walker's Point. I have to say, the view was spectacular, which added to the excitement of the moment. For those who have never been to Kennebunkport or by the Bush's family estate, you can catch a glimpse of it by stopping by Blowing Cave Park on Ocean Avenue, looking across the cove where the waves crash up against the shoreline. The scene is absolutely breathtaking. It wasn't long after parking that others began to join us, sitting on the hoods of their cars to take in the view. It was a great place to finally regroup, as well as relax for the first time since we had left Brenham.

Approximately fifteen minutes before 10:00 a.m., we got back into the car and made our way around to the entrance. Upon arrival, we pulled up to the guard shack, where we were greeted by the attendant, as well as the Secret Service. I will never forget our formal announcement to the President: "Sir, your ice cream is here!" There's nothing like having a special prized possession to open the gate to the President, but Homemade Vanilla will do that—every time.

"Sir, your ice cream is here!"
—Attendant to President George Bush

We made our way over to a small white house, then we were guided up the stairs to the second floor where we found President Bush in his study. There was a crazy level of excitement and anticipation; I remember immediately thinking I was standing in front of the former President of the United States, and yet, I felt like I was visiting an old friend. He warmly greeted us and proceeded to spend the next fifteen minutes or so talking about Blue Bell, the Kruses, and life in general. He also reminded us of just how blessed we were to live in the greatest country in the world, to which we agreed. As quick as our visit started, the President was interrupted by a call he had been waiting on. While we thought our visit had come to an end, he instead commented that Mrs. Bush also wanted to visit with us and asked his associates to escort us to the main house.

Making our way, we were once again taken in by the beauty of the surroundings and humbly appreciated the opportunity to see the view from the balcony of their home. The first lady greeted us with a good old Texas hello and invited us in. "Hello, I'm Ricky Dickson, and this is my wife, Anita," to which she responded, "I know who you are, you brought us ice cream. Now come on in, and please, call me Barbara." Her enthusiasm and warmth were exactly what I expected.

We made our way to their living room, and as we visited, I thought about how surreal this whole experience had become. There were times it felt as if we were visiting our grandparents, whom we hadn't seen for ages. Yet, reality would check back as I looked at the pictures that adorned the room, some displaying their grandchildren but other photos displaying dignitaries from all over the world.

As we wrapped up our time together, Barbara asked if we wanted to have some fun. She said that often, tourist boats would pull up into the cove to try and get a glimpse of who was here on the grounds. She called them "Bush watchers." She said, "If we go out on the deck, it could really throw them. They know who I am, but they won't know who you are. Let's give them something to talk about."

How could we turn that offer down? So, we politely accepted, and off we went. As we made our way through the house, she stopped and pointed to a particular painting hanging on the wall and followed by asking our opinion on if it went with the décor of the room. Before either Anita or I could answer, she said Putin, *the President of Russia*, had given it to them, and she wasn't really sure if it went there or not. Talk about being brought back to reality.

Out on the beautiful deck that circled the exterior of the home and faced the ocean down below, I could only imagine the beautiful sunrises that were painted across the sky every morning from this most amazing place. Looking out across the water, as predicted, there were about half a dozen boats anchored in position, those on board with binoculars in hand. Let the speculative conversation begin! There were also a few cars across the cove in the parking area where we had been about an hour earlier. I didn't have the heart to tell the First Lady that just an hour earlier, we had been part of the Bush watcher fan club. It's amazing how our special gift was the key that opened the door for this special time. I wondered if those we had met across the cove were still there. If so, there was no telling where their conversation would take them next.

After our visit with the First Lady, we had a tour of the rest of the property, including the workout facility, and took turns riding the President's Segways around the compound. We finally made our way back to the small white house, where we started to finish our visit with President Bush. Our final time together included watching a few home movies of the grandkids. The highlight reel included a mock press conference, where the grandchildren dressed up as reporters and the President and First Lady sat in lawn chairs wearing full-body T-shirts. The President had a cartoon male bodybuilder on his, while Barbara had a cartoon of a female in a bikini—you know the shirts I'm talking about. The President also had a hat that included a duck bill, web feet, and a tail. They were just people—two grandparents doing whatever it took to make their grandkids happy. It was an incredible time together and moments we will never forget.

Soon, we made our way back to our car to take pictures and say our goodbyes. The President agreed to our picture request but wanted to include his speed boat in the background, which was cutting across the ocean waves out in front of us. He said, "See that boat? That one's mine, and I was able to get it up to 70 mph last week." I asked him how the Secret Service felt about that, to which he just smiled.

It was so much to process. Meeting the President and the First Lady and experiencing the beauty of Walker's Point was incredible enough, but discovering how down-to-earth and accepting they were was really something. I mean the commander in chief of the greatest country in the world and his wife had opened up their home to Anita and me. It was a profound experience.

It dawned on me: If an earthly man could command so much respect from me, then how much more in awe should I be when I encounter the King of Kings? I can only imagine! At any moment, day or night, each of us has the opportunity to visit the Creator of the universe. His love goes beyond anything we can comprehend, and He wants us to come just as we are!

During our time with the Bushes, I quickly realized that it wasn't so much about what I wore, but about just being me. (Anita had, of course, been right.) God is also like that. He wants what is on the inside, He wants our heart. We tend to judge the outside, without breaking open the inside.

GEORGE BUSH

August 7, 2007

Dear Ricky,

Thanks for your note, but the pleasure was all ours. You know, of course, that we Bushes are great Blue Bell fans; and along you came and so thoughtfully replenished our supply. I'm glad you came out to see us at this Point we love so much.

Please give my warm regards to all Kruses.

Sincerely

G Bu

Mr. Ricky Dickson
General Sales Manger
Blue Bell Creameries, L.P.
Post Office Box 1807
Brenham, TX 77834-1807

WALKER'S POINT, POST OFFICE BOX 492, KENNEBUNKPORT, MAINE 04046
PHONE (207) 967-5800 / FAX (207) 967-0255

God wants my heart and will take me just as I am. I tend to get caught up in playing church instead of stripping everything away and praising God for who He is and for what He has done. When you can cut through what is defined as religion and break into a relationship, you will be able to recognize His voice and rest in His presence. As excited as I might have been to meet the President, how much more should I be about spending time with the Creator of the universe? It's an amazing gift that is available for all who believe, and the pathway to this gift comes through His Son.

Amazing Grace how sweet the sound
That saved a wretch like me.
I once was lost but now I'm found
Was blind, but now I see

There was something incredibly special about that day, and when I think back, I realize it was centered around another phone call, but this time, I was the one calling. I also realized that as special as the gift of ice cream might have been, I believe it was the relationship with the Kruse family that opened the door to their home. The gift of ice cream just made it extra special for them.

In the same way, the gift of eternal life in Heaven is given by God Almighty through His Son on the cross. The difference is He is there waiting to have a personal relationship with you, and all you have to do is open the door.

Revelations 3:20 says:

Look! I stand at the door and knock. If you hear my voice and

open the door, I will come in, and we will share a meal together
as friends.

Our gift to Him is our heart! It's the start of a relationship that will last much longer than a bowl of ice cream on a hot summer day. Instead, it will last forever, but you must first accept and believe. If you don't already have this relationship, what's keeping you from opening the door?

10

A "Meal"-ion Reasons to Feel Blessed!

I have always loved the change in seasons. Throughout the country, there is a distinct separation from spring to summer to fall to winter, with each period celebrated as it enters and then exits. Growing up in San Antonio, though, this seemed to only happen twice a year. There was summer, then the few weeks that fell in between Thanksgiving and Christmas. Sure, there were brief periods of time in January and February that resembled winter, but the winds of fast-moving cold fronts seemed to disappear as fast as they arrived.

Even so, there was something special about the first signs of cooler weather. The atmosphere seemed to trigger something inside, reminding us that the holiday season was just around the corner. Mixed in with the crazy experience of shopping for loved ones and garnishing the house with an array of lights and landscape figurines, the fall and winter traditions most always included bragging rights about everyone's favorite college and/or pro football teams.

Bragging rights from week to week separated the elite from the wannabes, yet school pride was defended no matter who you rooted for. The debate seemed to always dominate weekday water cooler discussions and would crescendo around one of my favorite holiday seasons—Thanksgiving!

As significant as this pigskin dialogue was to the Thanksgiving season, the main event was always centered around the dinner table, joining family and friends to celebrate our many blessings. In preparation for this important holiday tradition, gathering together for the annual feast is as close to gluttony as any Baptist potluck casserole Sunday night celebration can be.

What potentially was considered to be our nation's "national bird" instead ended up as the traditional sacrifice that takes center stage at almost every family gathering nationwide. While the bald eagle soars high above most of our fifty great states, turkeys are being basted and seasoned to everyone's desired taste in kitchens below. Whether your fowl friend is smoked, baked, or fried, a Thanksgiving meal without turkey as the centerpiece seems un-American. (I've actually never been a big turkey fan, but even so, turkey is still a must!)

Surrounding this main attraction is its ever-present supporting cast of side dishes, all fighting for attention: dressing, mashed potatoes, candied yams, green bean casserole, creamed corn, cranberry salad, and fresh hot homemade rolls (dripping in butter). Did I forget to mention the gravy? Growing up in a large family, the traditional Thanksgiving dinner drew all my cousins from both sides of the family tree together and included our own version of touch football in the host's front yard. Instead of each family going head-to-head, my dad and my uncle would mix up siblings so no pre-strategy trick plays could be implemented. The tradition was also a great way for the cooks in the kitchen to prepare in a calm environment while the rest of us built up an even greater appetite.

The games never really amounted to anything serious as far as injuries but bragging rights spilled over until the real games began on TV. Along with the pigskin battles taking place, it was also a tradition to have a card table or two set up with the annual 1000-piece jigsaw puzzle challenge to commence. It was waiting for anyone willing, no matter their age. A tradition that continues with my family today. Surrounded by those you loved the most, Thanksgiving truly is a special time of year.

Oh, how I love the holiday season to include the bounty of our dinner finally!

As wonderful as my savory culinary masterpiece is, I can't help but camp out by the dessert table. Although my mind has given much thought to the main course, I've carved out even more room for the dessert.

My dilemma: Do I select one piece of pie from the endless options available, or do I create a sampler platter that will require both hands to carry? Either way, I need to make room for a large scoop of vanilla ice cream.

But, not just *any* vanilla ice cream.

For all of us at Blue Bell, the decision is obvious. There is only one vanilla ice cream worthy enough to rest atop Mom's cherry cobbler or Grandma's special pecan pie—Blue Bell's Homemade Vanilla. Since its creation in 1969, it's been the cornerstone of our business, and is the go-to flavor for times such as these. It's an important member of our family, and perfect for any occasion, whether it be the good … or not so good.

As important as the dessert table became for our family, the focus of Thanksgiving still remains with the turkey. In our house, we were traditionalists, meaning we always had a large bird, baked to perfection. The only time we strayed from the always-consistent ever-reliable oven was when I thought it would be fun one year to fry the turkey. Frying a turkey had become the new thing to do, and anyone brave enough to attempt this deep fry madness received the instant culinary chef's award for bravery. I was eager to accept the challenge and ready for the praise that would soon follow.

My only problem was I didn't own a deep fryer, so I decided to give it a try on top of our stove. (You can already see where this is going!) Using two wooden, long-handle spoons, I carefully positioned the Italian-dressing-injected bird over the makeshift pan, filled with hot vegetable oil that was waiting for the full immersion to begin. Anita pulled the kids away from the potential Thanksgiving bonfire and repeated those parental words, "Are you sure you know what you're doing?" In her mind, "Project Fried Turkey" was on the launch pad ten seconds before a potential liftoff.

Before I could strategize how to lower the turkey into the hot oil jacuzzi, the right handle on the "wooden" spoon snapped, and the last words I heard from our feathered friend were "Cannon Ball." Fortunately, with the quick thinking of my better two-thirds (my wife), the mess was immediately controlled, even before the kids could dial 911. Needless to say, we never tried that craziness again. Smoked or baked have been our go-to ever since.

As it turns out, turkeys are a must, no matter how they are prepared. Even Clark Griswold from the movie *National Lampoon's Christmas Vacation* can pull his holiday magic, convincing Cousin Catherine her masterpiece is the best. *Even if it was a little dry.*

WHO'S THE TURKEY?

According to the United States Department of Agriculture, over forty-six million turkeys are eaten each year during Thanksgiving. To add to that statistic, according to the National Turkey Federation, approximately 88 percent of Americans eat turkey on Thanksgiving, which means roughly 293.3 million people will eat turkey in 2023. Yet, the USDA claims that number is significantly lower, reporting only 25 percent of all Americans eat turkey on Thanksgiving Day. No matter which statistic you choose to believe, the turkey seems to be the main guest of honor throughout the entire land.

As much as I enjoy hunting in the outdoors, I have never harvested a turkey of my own. But I know the actual art of calling in a turkey can be exciting, especially if you can get a nice, bearded Tom to respond to your invitational call. It's exciting, that is, if you are in a position to defend yourself from an unexpected attack. Normally, if you are calling in a turkey, you're in full camo, positioned out of harm's way. Then, the magic begins when the hunter tries a varied number of calls to see if there are any participants eager for action. The key is to make a sound that is inviting and non-threatening. Thinking I am a pretty good caller, I decided to try and talk to my feathered friends one day on a walk but I must have said something over the line. If you're not actually hunting, coming face to face with a turkey would be a lot less likely unless you lived in the country or were to visit the local zoo.

Ironically, Anita and I recently moved into a neighborhood that included the usual squirrels, rabbits, and an occasional armadillo. In addition, we were also blessed with racoons, opossums, whitetail deer, and yes ... a few curious turkeys. None of these creatures would be considered dangerous unless provoked but talking to them seemed natural and almost encouraging. Or so I thought ...

As embarrassing as this example is to share, this encounter best describes this vulnerable situation I found myself in this past spring. Months after the Thanksgiving and Christmas holidays had taken their toll, I decided to put my annual New Year's resolution into practice.

With the anticipation of retirement on the horizon, the reminder of "eating right and exercising" became a battle cry in preparation for the next phase of my life. Okay, it also was the stern words from my physician during my annual physical. It seemed that after forty-two-plus years of a steady ice cream diet, my sugar level was becoming the topic of discussion, and medication was his first solution. Not mine.

It was also the time when I realized, outside of Thanksgiving and maybe Christmas, all things in moderation should now include ice cream and could be determined by the size of the plate or bowl and not the scoop. A large bowl made the scoop appear small, demanding a second or third just to seem like you were eating something. I have since learned that a 3-ounce cup is the perfect portion control for anyone trying to learn the basic steps of moderation.

With portion control now in play, the second half of this wise advice came the dreaded word: *exercise.* For some, this comes easy, but the kind of exercise that would make a difference for me would require discipline and commitment. Trying to make the decision between taking medication or changing my lifestyle was a tough one, but one that needed to be made. Over the next few months, I changed my morning routine and began walking approximately two miles at a brisk pace. My goal was not to try and win a marathon but to walk far and fast enough to achieve the desired goal.

With a new mindset and a routine that seemed to become manageable, I set out one beautiful spring morning with Anita to walk our neighborhood. Not realizing my pace had picked up from the last time we had both walked together, I found myself taking off then slowing down to keep the same pace and walk together. The struggle between quality time and accelerated heartbeats became the topic of discussion, and finally, Anita said to go for it … quality time could come after the finish line.

With those words of support and acceptance, off I went. Cool breeze in the air and David Phelps's music in my earbuds, I took off. At about the mile-and-a-half mark is where this story takes an interesting turn.

As I made my way down the back street of the neighborhood, I noticed a group of turkeys in a vacant lot. Feeling like a turkey (which seems to come naturally), I let out a bellowing "GOBBLE" to announce my presence and grab the attention of these fair-feathered friends. Now, I have been told that to be a good turkey caller, you need to understand what you are saying and the meaning behind each sound. I am not really sure what I said, but "Tom," the proud male in the group with his back toward me, flared out his feathers and slowly turned my direction and declared war.

At first, I was amazed at my ability to speak turkey so clearly, let alone fire up this little guy, but as I made my way down the street toward him, he was not amused. He decided to meet me halfway. Now, I've been around turkeys before, but not in a direct "man to bird" show-down. I'm not sure what I said to him to get him all worked up, but I wasn't about to repeat it. Our distance closed within twenty yards, and I began to generate other words of choice, hoping to keep the distance from narrowing. My fast-paced walk changed into a jog, then a full-out old-man run, until I felt the battle had been avoided, leaving super "Tom" with all his dignity with the ladies that he had left.

Speaking of ladies left behind, as I made my way up the last hill to our house, it dawned on me that Anita had to come right by those same turkeys, and the confrontation could potentially have a different outcome. I immediately turned around and went back to save my bride from this turkey disaster. As soon as I rounded the corner on one end of the street, Anita began coming up on the opposite end. Turkey "Tom" was waiting in the middle.

As I approached, he turned and recognized my voice as I cried out a warning to Anita. Once again, he made his way straight for me, this time with battle on his mind. From the safe twenty yards that once separated us, the distance became more like ten, then five. With nothing but a garage door opener in hand and a bad turkey call, I tried desperately to keep away from the sharp spurs that "Tom" could try to use as weapons. He proceeded to fly up and down, hissing and cackling to frighten me away. I never knew a Butterball could hiss like that, but he was determined to keep me away. I repeatedly tried to turn and look for an object of defense, but I didn't trust turning my back on this fowl-feathered enemy. Trying to keep him distracted, I yelled at Anita to get a stick or rock and try to shoo him away.

Now, I have to admit, at this time, from one male ego to the other, this turkey was kicking my butt. What happened to all that training I had been doing? How had man fallen to such a place? Was this being filmed by the neighbors with the anticipation of winning $10,000 on *America's Funniest Videos?* And then it happened ... with one small stick in hand, my beautiful bride proceeded to hold turkey "Tom" at bay, screaming, "Leave my husband alone! Leave my husband alone!"

Well, I must admit, her actions defused this confrontation, and turkey "Tom" finally waddled back to the hens that were on the sidelines cheering him on. Anita escorted me, with all dignity lost, back up the hill, encouraging and thanking me for coming back to her rescue. After that experience, I soon found out that springtime was mating season for this Thanksgiving centerpiece, and whatever I said, it didn't settle well with this proud resident neighbor. He's one of the lucky ones.

For most turkeys, the odds of making it through the season could be slim, but there is one specific bird that is spared this oven sauna experience. It happens every year in Washington, D.C. One lucky turkey is chosen to be a guest at the party instead of the centerpiece of the main course.

The official "pardoning" of the White House turkey is an interesting tradition and one that has captured the imagination of many over the past two hundred years. This gallinaceous bird tradition can be traced back to Abraham Lincoln, who reportedly gave clemency to one lucky feathered friend back in 1865. But it wasn't until 1989 that President George H.W. Bush made the pardoning tradition official. Some swear it was actually a turkey that first coined the phrase, "I peck your pardon," while onlookers, when hearing the discussion, thought he cried out, "I beg your pardon." Either way, every year since then, one lucky turkey has been able to change their extremely anxious attitude to one of overwhelming gratitude, saving the use of their wishbone for another day.

FROM THE GARDEN TO THE CROSS

Thanksgiving dinner and pardoning are two critical events in history that take us back to the beginning of mankind. From the Garden of Eden, man was given the gift of choice, and even though turkey and dressing were not on the menu, Adam and Eve had an incredible selection of fruits and nuts to feast on for a lifetime. But with this gift of making one's own decisions came the price of consequences from each one, and we soon learned that the desire of "knowledge" trumped "everlasting life." This hunger for knowledge, as attractive as it might be, has led man down the road of destruction. From every generation since, man has tried but failed miserably to stay faithful to God, consistently getting caught in his selfish ways, followed by his selfish deeds. With no hope of breaking the cycle, this spiraling pattern eventually led to the greatest gift of all.

What became painfully obvious was that man could not save himself, and through God's love, Christ entered the world. His life not only taught us how to live on earth, but through His obedience, He took the sins of the world and nailed them to the cross and died to pay the price no man could pay. Christ's acceptance of the cross pardoned all those who simply turn their lives over to Him and trust Him as their personal Savior. Once again, mankind has the ability to choose, and everlasting life comes through Christ's blood on a tree.

> *6 When we were utterly helpless, Christ came at just the right time and died for us sinners. 7 Now, most people would not be willing to die for an upright person, though someone might perhaps be willing to die for a person who is especially good. 8 But God showed his great love for us by sending Christ to die for us while we were still sinners. 9 And since we have been made right in God's sight by the blood of Christ, he will certainly save us from God's condemnation. 10 For since our friendship with God was restored by the death of his Son while we were still his enemies, we will certainly be saved through the life of his Son.*
>
> *11 So now we can rejoice in our wonderful new relationship with God because our Lord Jesus Christ has made us friends of God.*
>
> —ROMANS 5:6–11

It is also interesting to see that right before Jesus walked down the road to the cross, the most important meal of thanksgiving was celebrated by His closest followers.

For the twelve disciples, this Passover meal had been a tradition, but the meaning of this specific meal would soon significantly change for generations to come. As Jesus and his disciples prepared for this meal, they gathered together to remember the Passover. This Passover meal was the oldest and most important festival in Judaism and was a time of reflection, praise, and celebration of how God delivered the Hebrews from slavery through the exodus from Egypt.

14 When the time came, Jesus and the apostles sat down together at the table.[a] 15 Jesus said, "I have been very eager to eat this Passover meal with you before my suffering begins. 16 For I tell you now that I won't eat this meal again until its meaning is fulfilled in the Kingdom of God."

17 Then he took a cup of wine and gave thanks to God for it. Then he said, "Take this and share it among yourselves. 18 For I will not drink wine again until the Kingdom of God has come."

19 He took some bread and gave thanks to God for it. Then he broke it in pieces and gave it to the disciples, saying, "This is my body, which is given for you. Do this in remembrance of me."

20 After supper he took another cup of wine and said, "This cup is the new covenant between God and his people—an agreement confirmed with my blood, which is poured out as a sacrifice for you.[b]

—LUKE 22:14–20

Ever since that day, the Lord's supper is taken regularly as a sacrament by Christians all over the world as a remembrance of Christ himself. This time though, this meal was to remember God's grace for all mankind.

Grace is an amazing gift! It is so hard to comprehend God's love for us by allowing Christ to take our place for the sins that we have committed. Sins that have been part of our DNA since the decision made in the garden thousands of years ago. This amazing forgiveness came with a price, and by placing faith in Him, all of our sins—past, present, and future—are forgiven. Each and every sin was nailed to that cross that day..

Unfortunately, we so often treat this grace as an entitlement, forgetting the price that was paid. A battle rages within each of us. With the gift of choice comes the responsibility of seeking God in all we do, both in the good times as well as the bad. Ironically, it seems that the more difficult our times become, the quicker we are brought back to this starting line compared to times in our lives when things are good.

Comparing myself to "Tom" the turkey, life seems pretty normal until I hear the oven turn on to preheat. Then, as the temperature rises, I try to escape the situation by using the "my way" ideas as a go-to for my solutions. It's not until I have surrendered all my ways before the Lord and allowed God to take full control that the peace that surpasses all understanding takes root. In the end, every thought, every breath, and every step of faith are all for His glory—I should recognize this from the beginning of every day, no matter how painful it might seem.

Although Thanksgiving's mega-meal has garnered much attention over the years, the true meaning of the Thanksgiving season is really centered on God's unwavering love, spending time with family and friends, making new memories, and reflecting on the sacrifice that took place for our pardon. It's also about reflecting on how blessed we are to live in such an amazing country. For these truths, we can never forget.

So, with each Thanksgiving, put keto on the shelf, walk a few extra laps around the neighborhood, and make sure spandex is invited to the party. New memories are waiting to be made. It's also good to take in a football game or two, as long as the house is not too divided.

Most importantly, remember, for those in Christ, there will one day be an amazing banquet prepared for us in Heaven, and at that celebration, there will be pardons given out for more than just one turkey. The price has been paid.

I can only imagine what that spread of food will consist of, yet even more importantly, the celebration of praise that will last much longer than Mom's award-winning coconut cream pie.

> [6] *Then I heard what sounded like a great multitude, like the roar*
> *of rushing waters and like loud peals of thunder, shouting:*
>
> *"Hallelujah!*
> *For our Lord God Almighty reigns.*
> [7] *Let us rejoice and be glad*
> *and give him glory!*
> *For the wedding of the Lamb has come,*
> *and his bride has made herself ready.*
> [8] *Fine linen*, bright and clean,*
> *was given her to wear."*
>
> [9] *Then the angel said to me, "Write this: Blessed are those*
> *who are invited to the wedding supper of the Lamb!" And*
> *he added, "These are the true words of God."*
>
> —REVELATION 19: 6-9

---

*Fine linen stands for the righteous acts of God's holy people.

11

What Have You Created for Me Lately?

The year was 1941, or was it '51? Actually, no one knows for sure, but it was a time when our R&D team decided to leave the comforts of the crowded chocolate-and-vanilla world and concoct a flavor that would become the talk of the town. Ironically, it still makes its way into conversation today when consumers ask me, "What's the craziest flavor you have ever made?"

Faced with this "cue-cumbersome" task, our experts thought long and hard, not eliminating even the craziest of ideas. This limited edition flavor didn't necessarily need to be the "bread and butter" of the overall ice cream program, but it did need to be somewhat of a big "dill." So came the creation of Dill Pickle 'n Cream. Talk about an attention-getter; combining pickles with ice cream might have started a new craze, or at least become the perfect solution to satisfy the midnight labor cravings. I know both pickles and ice cream top that particular list, but it seemed to have the opposite effect.

From what I understand, a single, three-gallon production run was all that was ever produced, and apparently, all that was needed.

I can't help but believe this flavor was created more to generate discussion around the dinner table than requests for "more please," and even though it didn't become a classic, it achieved the goal of getting attention.

The second misfire was almost as bad, but the flavor seemed to have a lot more promise. I still remember the introduction of Peanut Butter and Jelly. It was a creamy peanut butter ice cream with a strawberry ripple that actually tasted really good but failed miserably. Maybe we should have cut the crust off first ... just kidding. As a company, we are always trying to think outside the box, but lunch boxes should have been off-limits.

Today, vanilla and chocolate still reign as America's top choices when buying ice cream, but it's the unique, think-outside-of-the-box combinations that seem to generate the most buzz from our consumers. Since those early days, creating exciting new flavors has been part of our mystique, giving consumers something to look forward to when walking down the freezer aisle with Christmas-like anticipation.

We introduced Cookies 'n Cream in the early eighties, and it soon replaced Dutch Chocolate as our number two best seller. Since then, flavors created with variations of cookies and cookie dough pieces have remained popular. More recently, cake pieces have made their way onto the scene, giving our artistic team opportunities for even more great flavor options.

As far as Dill Pickle 'n Cream ... Unless it's a pregnant woman or someone with a passion for cucumbers, I don't believe many today would "relish" the idea of its return. However, with the way trends come and go, we'll leave the door "a jar," just in case.

THE CREATION OF ICE CREAM

I am often asked (right after what my favorite flavor of ice cream is), how you come up with so many flavors? Who's the mastermind behind each one, and who decides which flavors make it into the lineup each season? Each of these questions and many more are great and really get to the heart of what we do. It's a tough job, but someone has to do it.

Before we can look at flavor selection, it's important to first know what exactly ice cream is. Let's start with the basics. What defines this frozen magical treat, and why are there so many prices, shapes, and sizes to choose from? From the occasional novelist to the true connoisseur, the makeup of ice cream can be broken down into two basic components: the percent of butterfat added into the mix and the amount of air that is incorporated into the mix when it is being churned.

Merriam-Webster defines ice cream as "a sweet flavored frozen food containing cream or butterfat and usually eggs," but to be legally labeled ice cream, it must have dairy products. Sounds simple enough, yet today we are seeing a variety of attempts to challenge this definition by using plant-based alternatives as the fat source.

In the ice cream industry, there are a variety of textbooks that explain the basics of making ice cream and related products. For me, when referencing the complexity, I immediately refer to my original textbook, *Ice Cream,* Fourth Edition, by W.S. Arbuckle. From what I understand, there are now seven editions that have been edited due to technological changes, but I still gravitate back to the one I'm most familiar with when I explain the basics. He writes that ice cream is a frozen dairy food made by freezing a pasteurized mix with agitation to incorporate air and to ensure uniformity of consistency. In the United

States, ice cream is defined by U.S. Government standards. It must contain no less than 10 percent milk fat and 20 percent milk solids, except in the case of bulky flavors, the fat and total milk solids must not be less than 8 and 16 percent, respectively. It must weigh not less than 4.5 lb/gal; it must contain no more than 0.5 percent stabilizer; and it must contain not less than 1.6 lb of total food solids (TS) per gallon.

According to Jason Lexell, with Ice Cream Profits, it is also possible for ice cream retailers to sell products from other types of milk, such as goat milk, and to still label their products as ice cream.

Ice cream retailers who sell products with more than 1.4 percent egg yolk are required to call their product French ice cream or frozen custard. As stated by federal law, if a product is labeled ice cream, it must contain a minimum of 10 percent butterfat. Any less and the product would be classified as a frozen dairy dessert or some other type of frozen treat. To achieve this threshold, one can use any combination of milk, cream, buttermilk, and nonfat milk, as well as add ingredients including fruits or nuts and sugar. The second and equally important principle is the amount of overrun or air that is incorporated into the mix. Slices Concessions, an ice cream equipment specialist, defines overrun as the percent of ice cream that is air incorporated in the product during the freezing process to expand to make more product with less material. For example, when you make hard ice cream with an overrun of 30 percent, you have expanded the product by 30 percent.

Even though there are these two basic principles, there are hundreds of ways to interchange these components to create the variety of ice cream products that you find in stores and ice cream parlors today. A high butterfat, low overrun product will yield a heavier, denser product, whereas low butterfat, high overrun will be a lighter, less filling product.

So, what is the history of this amazing frozen treat?

We return back to Arbuckle's *Ice Cream,* Fourth Edition, and learn that ice cream probably came to the United States with the early English colonists. In 1851, the first wholesale ice cream industry in the United States was established in Baltimore, Maryland, by Jacob Fussell. Early plants were also established in St. Louis, New York, Washington, Chicago, and Cincinnati. The development of condensed dry milk, the introduction of the pasteurizer and homogenizer, improved freezers, and other processing equipment accompanied a slow growth in the industry until 1900. Making ice cream had been achieved by implementing this technology but keeping it frozen was a whole different story. Ice and salt helped with the freezing process, but only for a short period of time.

The ice cream soda was introduced in 1879; the ice cream cone in 1904; and the Eskimo Pie in 1921. Around 1920 the value of ice cream as an essential food was generally recognized, and the product has become unusually popular since that time. The development of improved refrigeration and transportation, low-temperature storage units for home, improved packaging, marketing through chain stores, and improved product standards have made ice cream widely available to the consumer.

So let the magic begin ...

Moving away from the more technical side of ice cream, we can now focus on the imagination of endless possibilities of flavors. Similar to keys on a piano, when the notes are combined in a certain way, a masterpiece is created. Some songs are one-hit wonders, but then there's that moment in time when everything comes together, and a new creation becomes an instant classic. Creating a new flavor can be fun and exciting, with ideas coming from the youngest to the oldest culinary connoisseur. The only requirement: "You have to think outside the carton." Sure, there are limitations of certain ingredients due to availability or cost, but combining fruits, baked goods, sauces, nuts, and other creative ingredients can open up the door for the potential new classic flavor(s) of the future.

For Blue Bell, flavors like Dutch Chocolate, Cookies 'n Cream, and Cookie Two Step top the list, with Buttered Pecan, Pralines 'n Cream, and Mint Chocolate Chip not far behind. But of course, the flavor that put Blue Bell on the map, hands down, is Homemade Vanilla. This creation, invented in 1969 by Howard Kruse, comes the closest to hand-cranked vanilla you can find anywhere. With Blue Bell only available in twenty-three states, it consistently ranks as one of the top-selling flavors in the country.

There is something magical about ice cream. For kids of all ages, ice cream has the power to transport you to somewhere in your past or create new memories for you in your future. It's a great way to celebrate a birthday or joyous occasion or help erase a bad day when things seem to go wrong. A friend to lean on in tough times or the perfect ending to a great day.

One of the greatest parts of my job is hearing from our consumers about the passion they have for a certain flavor of Blue Bell. It's almost as if we created it with them specifically in mind. Who am I to tell them anything different? The letters come from all over the country and from all ages, and it's the motivating ingredient to making sure we consistently do it right. Our mission is to "consistently meet the expectation that drives the passion" with each and every product we make. It's all we do, so we have to get it right every time.

The following are some of my favorite stories that bring this all together. Who better to have an ice cream wish list than children? Here are a few letters that have come from kids all over the country. I love their imagination and they prove there are no boundaries to where their creativity will take them.

Dear Mr. Blue Bell,

I've never experienced something so flavorful and mouth watering than your magnificent blue bell ice cream! That mint chocolate chip flavor will always make me happy when I'm down and joyful when I've got a frown. Everytime I eat it my eyes glow with joy and happiness even when I didn't know I could get any happier!

I'm 11 yrs. Old, and I'm turning 12 soon. My name is Hallie Joe and I'm a homeschooler who's favorite dessert is mint chocolate chip ice cream. One time my dad bought and offbrand of mint chocolate chip ice cream.

I'll give you five reasons why it was terriable:

1. *It's not made by professional Blue Bell people.*
2. *It wasn't even green it was white.*
3. *They had hardley any chocolate chips.*
4. *They were made of dark chocolate chips.*
5. *It was way too sweet and hard to scoop.*

Don't you see, I never want y'all to stop selling your fantastic icecream. Would you do me a huge favor and send me some mint chocolate chip? I would be so thankful and super happy!

Thank you Mr. Blue Bell!!

Love Hallie

* * *

Dear Blue Bell:

I am writing to tell you how much i love your ice cream. My favorite flavor is cookies and cream. I have 2 brothers and 1 sister and they love your ice cream, too. Do you make banana ice cream? I think you are really sweet.

Todd

* * *

To whom it may concern:

Hi, I made a new flavor of ice cream called Avocado. I think it sounds really good.

You could make it with lime ice cream as the base, and cookie dough as the pit in the middle.

It could increase sales because people would like it. It is also fun to try new things, even if they are not that great. I think it will be great, though!

You guys also have permission to use the ice cream name. I promise I will not sue you! Thank you so much for reading this. I hope you like it.

Sincerely, Jacob

* * *

Dear Blue Bell,

I have a sour flavor that will blow your hat's off. Sour cherry explosion.

Ingredients to make the ice cream: 1. Cherry ice cream. 2. Sliced cherries. 3. Sour candy. 4. Chocolate chips.

Love,
Sean

* * *

Dear Blue Bell,

Hi, I'm Zoey and I have created a new ice cream yes me! Okay, here is the idea. So the flavor is chocolate and has nutela and penut butter on it and whipped cream. The ice cream is called chocolate peanut. You don't have to put whipped cream on it it optinal.

-Zoey

Even though the majority of ice cream flavors that we sell each year are centered around the basics, like vanilla, chocolate, and cookies 'n cream, it's the "what is the new flavor" requests that peak our imaginations. There's no one better to open that door of endless concoctions than the innocence of a child. They will boldly speak their mind with the confidence of a contestant on *Iron Chef.*

There is so much we can learn from this confidence, especially when it comes to faith. What better example than what we read in Luke, when the disciples looked at children as a nuisance or a distraction from Jesus's ministry, and yet it was their innocent faith that represented total trust in the Savior they served.

> *15 One day some parents brought their little children to Jesus so He could touch and bless them. But when the disciples saw this, they scolded the parents for bothering Him.*
>
> *16 Then Jesus called for the children and said to the disciples, "Let the children come to me. Don't stop them! For the Kingdom of God belongs to those who are like these children. 17 I tell you the truth, anyone who doesn't receive the Kingdom of God like a child will never enter it."*
>
> —LUKE 18:15-17

As we come before the throne, we, too, are children of God and can approach Him with the same level of trust, knowing that He loves us more than we can ever comprehend.

1 John 5: 1-2 says it best:

> *Everyone who believes that Jesus is the Christ [a] has become a child of God. And everyone who loves the Father loves His*

children, too. ² We know we love God's children if we love God and obey His commandments.

By placing your faith and trust in Christ, you too become a new creation and, unlike Sour Cherry Explosion or Avocado, this creation will last for eternity. Unlike the standard flavors, we are all made unique and one of a kind. We are also all God's favorites and all He asks in return is our hearts.

> ¹⁶ *Jesus repeated the question: "Simon son of John, do you love me?"*
> *"Yes, Lord," Peter said, "you know I love you."*
> *"Then take care of my sheep," Jesus said.*
>
> —JOHN 21:16

12

Being a Fanatic

66 "Fanatic" isn't a word I typically use in my everyday language. However, the term seems to best describe many of us at the beginning of every football season. Young and old alike seem to leave all self-dignity and respect at the door when it comes to supporting their favorite teams. Personalized outward expressions ranging from face painting, color-coded wigs, and specially designed clothing are the norm as people shift into their altered-ego state of mind.

The other day, I was reminded of that fanatical phenomenon as I waited to board a plane in Chicago.

In a sea of mothers pushing crying babies, newlyweds embarking on life's new adventures, and soldiers returning from the call of duty came this Green Bay Packers fanatic. "Sports Fan Joe," as I'll call him, entered the terminal modeling a green-and-khaki wardrobe with enough Green Bay bling to light a runway. Topping it off (literally) was a specially crafted straw hat adorned with a large block of cheese. On the triangular Styrofoam piece of cheddar, read the words "Texas Cheesehead."

I thought to myself, What would drive someone to that degree of loyalty, other than being a 100 percent die-hard fanatic of his favorite football team? I guess no matter how you cut it, you gotta love his passion. There's a little fanaticism in all of us. Although it sounds intense, it just means a person is passionate about something without resolve. Whether it's sports, cars, or spending time with family, everyone has something they enjoy to the fullest. Fortunately, for us, it's as simple as ice cream.

Which reminds me of a story that even Sports Fan Joe would appreciate.

A recent Tweet from Evergreen, Colorado, reported a bear (yes, a bear) ripped apart a local homeowner's garage door, opened their freezer, and stole a BRAND-NEW half gallon of Ultimate Neapolitan Ice Cream. The Tweet continued, "Blue Bell is indeed the best-tasting ice cream in the country, and the word has definitely spread." For this family, it was obviously *unbearable.*

I've met many people throughout my career and am always amazed by the number of Blue Bell fanatics out there. They range anywhere from first-time samplers to those who've eaten our ice cream since childhood and remain loyal to this day. This was never so evident than when we returned to the market in the fall of 2015. For over four months, our loyal consumers waited patiently for our return while we worked diligently, making the necessary changes to our manufacturing plants. With limited funds and to be transparent, we relied heavily on our newly developed social media to give updates and keep our customers informed. The support and comments were overwhelming.

As we slowly returned to the market after Labor Day, consumers greeted our reentry with open arms, and we were very humbled. In some locations, there were lines of loyal fans with spoons in hand, stretching from the ice cream aisle all the way to the front of the store, with the heightened anticipation of the return of their favorite flavors. I would say it was the most humbling experience I have had in my forty-three years with Blue Bell. Their loyalty and support renewed our strength to be the best we could possibly be and instilled a stronger commitment to excellence than ever before. We returned with a very simple "Thank You" campaign for our customers. Impassioned fans are a never-ending source of gratitude, and I believe we're fortunate to have the world's best cheering section. Whether you're a "Packer Backer" or another kind of fanatic, any season can be a win-win if it ends with a Super Bowl ... of Blue Bell, that is.

The driving force behind the passion for Blue Bell can come out of nowhere and convert the most converted introvert into the leader of the revolution. I am constantly reminded of this by the letters our consumer relations department receives on a daily basis. There are too many stories to cover in this book, but I do have a variety of favorites that really give you the flavor of the true-blue Blue Bell fan.

The first came to us in an unmarked envelope, with a direct message that didn't mince words ... or should I say letters. At the top of this anonymous ransom note was a picture of cows out in a field and then the following message:

We got UR cows
Bring back Cantaloupe n Cream
or else.

At the bottom of the ransom note was a picture of a hamburger. The writer went to a lot of trouble to send this intimidating message but didn't realize the cows in the picture weren't our cows. We could tell because they weren't wearing the right "Jerseys."

Another letter that caught my attention came to me around Christmas time. It was the day before Christmas, and I decided to run by the office and check emails. I noticed a letter in my inbox from a law firm in Dallas. Bah humbug was my initial thought. Seriously, who sends out a lawsuit at Christmas. Maybe it was fan mail or even better yet, new flavor recommendations? Well, I was right with both theories (kind of).

The letter read as follows:

Blue Bell Creameries
Consumer Relations
Brenham, Texas 77834

Re: The End of an ERA

Dear Sir or Madam:

Attached is a draft of a Plaintiff's Original Petition

Before this unfortunate pleasantness spins out of control, this matter can be resolved for the following consideration: Delivery to the undersigned at the above-mentioned address of a gallon of Spiced Pumpkin and Pecan ice cream on the Friday of each and every week between December 24, 2010, and Friday, January 28, 2011.

I look forward to the receipt of said items post haste.

Oh …. And Happy Holidays.

Very truly yours,

Larry Nelson

THE PEOPLE OF THE GREAT STATE INDISTRICT COURT OF TEXAS,

Plaintiff

V.

DALLAS COUNTY, TEXAS BLUE BELL CREAMERIES, INC

Defendant _____ JUDICIAL DISTRICT

PLAINTIFF'S ORIGINAL PETITION

THE PEOPLE OF THE GREAT STATE OF TEXAS ("Plaintiff") file this Original Petition against Blue Bell Creameries, Inc. ("Blue Bell" or Defendant") as follows:

1. Discovery will be conducted under Level 2 of Tex.R.Civ.P.190.1.

2. Plaintiff's are residents of the Great State of Texas residing from the piney woods of East Texas to the sandy shores of South Padre to the rugged plains of West Texas and all locales in between.

3. Blue Bell is a corporation duly incorporated under the laws of the State of Texas with its principal place of business in Brenham, Texas. Defendant may be served with process through any of its spokes cows located in or near Brenham, Texas.

4. Jurisdiction and venue are proper in this Court pursuant to Tex, Civ, Prac, &Rem.C. 15.002 (Vernon 2012) in that all or a substantial part of this cause of action arose in Dallas County, Texas, and the amount in controversy is in excess of the minimum jurisdictional limits of this court.

Background Facts

1. Defendant is in the business of providing all sorts of delicious with an emphasis on dairy products, specifically, but not limited to, ice

cream and ice cream products". The purpose of said products and the distribution thereof is to induce Plaintiff, the People of the Great State of Texas to partake thereof and through clever marketing and emphasizing a product which includes natural ingredients to induce Plaintiff to continue to purchase Defendant's product to finically enrich Defendant and to enslave Plaintiffs to continue to partake of Defendant's products. To this end, and to further accomplish Defendants purpose, from time to time, Defendant releases special ice cream flavors. In or about 2005, Blue Bell released a product called "Wedding Cake Ice Cream." To define said product as "divine" would be an understatement. In truth and in fact, the product "wedding Cake Ice Cream" was God apologizing for inventing brussels sprouts. However, Defendant only issued said product on a limited release, it has not re-released said product and said product is not even listed in the Defendants current or limited release of product lines. The purpose of this nefarious conduct was in truth and in fact, to cause a greater addiction to Defendants products and cause Plaintiff, the People of the Great State of Texas to purchase other products from Defendant which said Plaintiff may not have been willing or able to procure with the vainglorious hope that other flavors would excel to the level of Wedding Cake Ice Cream.

2. Therefore, in or about October of 2010, Defendant continued in its nefarious plot enslave Plaintiff, the People of the Great State of Texas, to become addicted to Defendant's products by releasing a new product called Spiced Pumpkin and Pecan Ice Cream. ("SPPIC"). SPPIC was a flavor so grand, so enticing that it was designed to induce Plaintiff to leave their employment, cast aside

their spouses, forget their gym memberships all for the purpose of tasting one last spoon full of SPPIC. In Defendant's press release regarding SPPIC, Defendant clearly stated: "This is a recipe we have been working on for quite some time …. The sugar-coated pecans and cinnamon-honey praline sauce are what set this pumpkin-based ice cream apart from all the rest…" The response to SPPIC was immediate and overwhelming. And as quickly as it appeared on the local grocery store shelves… it vanished as quickly as Aunt Matilda's flatulence during Hurricane Rita.

3. As expected, the response to the removal of SPPIC caused Plaintiff severe mental anguish and emotional distress. Persons who reside in Texas and yet attend Oklahoma University engaged in gnashing of teeth. Aggies from Texas A&M University laid down their sabers, abandoned their barn yards and named Bessie the cow to replace Reveille as their mascot. Even graduates from the Harvard of the South, the University of Texas, paused in our plans to take over the world to mourn the loss of SPPIC. Plaintiff made a demand upon Defendant to return these flavors to its regular rotation, but Defendant wholly failed and refused to comply.

The letter continued on and on, but it was apparent they loved our ice cream.

Boy, talking about getting hooked on a flavor during the holiday season, only to have it discontinued. This is probably the greatest challenge for our marketing department. Which flavors to return to the following year's lineup, and which ones to retire. Obviously, we needed to make a phone call and try and work ourselves out of this mess. The lack of Spiced Pumpkin Pecan's presence in the stores meant no presents at all for these plaintiffs, too, and impossible to gift wrap as well.

One of our more bizarre situations revolved around a pint of Bride's Cake in a Walmart store in Louisiana. In 2017, Blue Bell introduced two exciting flavors that were centered around weddings. After all, what goes better with a wedding cake than ice cream? In May of that year, both Bride's Cake and Groom's Cake made it onto shelves all across the Blue Bell selling area. Groom's Cake was a luscious chocolate ice cream with chocolate cake pieces and chocolate-coated strawberry hearts, surrounded by swirls of strawberry sauce and chocolate icing. A flavor that would keep the "runaway bride" at the altar for sure. Bride's Cake, on the other hand, was a masterful combination of almond ice cream with white cake pieces, surrounded by a rich amaretto cream cheese icing swirl. Who needs a wedding cake when you have these two amazing flavors? Groom's Cake was accepted overall, but Bride's Cake became the talk of the town and to say it exceeded expectations would be a major understatement.

This flavor was especially popular in Louisiana, where an almond-base cake flavor was the standard, and Blue Bell had matched this amazing taste to perfection. The demand grew so strong that it rivaled our number one flavor, Homemade Vanilla, as the top-selling flavor in total unit sales. We couldn't make it fast enough to meet the demand, and it became the "Where's Waldo" flavor that consumers were searching for in stores everywhere.

The demand grew so strong that in one supermarket in Louisiana, two shoppers both grabbed the last pint of Bride's Cake at the same time, and neither would let go. This led to a shouting match, followed by the local authorities to step in to separate them. We knew then that this was a flavor that needed to return—every year.

From one of the universities in the state, we received this letter from a college student:

Dear Blue Bell Creameries,

I'm writing to you because I am overwhelmed with joy at the recent discovery of one of your products.

Imagine this...

You're a twenty-something-year-old browsing the ice cream coolers at Walmart. The sale on Blue Bell catches your eye and your face is now pressed to the glass. (Corona virus was not yet at its current epidemic state.) Your health-conscious, more responsible boyfriend calling your name is muffled in the background.

There it is. The things dreams are made of. A big, bright yellow, ½ gallon carton of what Jesus wished his last meal was made of. None other than Banana Pudding Ice Cream. Now, I'm a Florida native. I do not claim to be from the South. Florida only dreams of claiming rights to being "Southern." But there I was, 5 years old again. In some middle-of-nowhere county in Georgia, at my grandmother's house, in my swimsuit, running through the sprinkler. She shelled pecans on her wrap-around porch. I finished my summer day with enough banana pudding to keep Jello-O and Nilla Wafers in business, maybe even during the apocalypse. Only to wake up and do it all over again the next day.

Flash back to reality. The glass is fogged up from my hot and heavy breathing. However, being the young, broke college kid that I am, I must prioritize the space in my fridge. And my pizza rolls and bottle of water were currently occupying the entirety of what would be the equivalent of a studio apartment space you could call my freezer. I walked away from the ice cream, kinda like the way I walk out of the animal shelter once a week, hoping to buy yet another dog. Empty-handed with tears welling up in my eyes.

Fast forward to 2 days ago. It's about 2:00 am. I just got out of my 12-hour serving shift at a theme park restaurant. And I need something to ease the pain in my feet and back. But mostly in my soul from all the absolute ignorance of the general public. Looking for something sweet, I wander back into the ice cream aisle. This time, I glance over to an end cap freezer, and I swear Handel's Hallelujah Chorus plays over the loudspeaker. Trumpets and all. There it is. Blue Bell Banana Pudding ice cream. This time, in a size willing to squeeze into the corner of my limited-space freezer.

I bought 2.

Definitely ate one in my car before I drove home.

No shame.

Now that this letter is longer and more passionate than any college essay I've ever written, I want to conclude with gratitude. For making my dreams come true. Not only in making the ice cream flavor of my dreams, but for making sizes for every occasion. Before 2 weeks ago, I didn't even know such a beautiful thing could happen. (Banana pudding has an ice cream flavor.) Now, I'll never go back. I can't even pretend that I want to use my Kitchen Aid ice cream maker attachment that I just got for Christmas. I just know nothing will compare to the new love I have found.

I just wanted to let you all at Blue Bell know that I am forever grateful for giving me the opportunity to experience this product. It's perfect in all its yellow carton glory. And obviously, the Nilla wafers are the best part. I will continue to purchase this product for as long as you allow. My only wish is that you inform me before pulling it off shelves so that I can purchase a large enough storage unit to fit 4 utility freezers and buy the entire stock from my local stores.

In short, y'all made an amazing product, and I just might be Banana Pudding's biggest fan.

Love,
Rachel

Then, there were more touching stories that started out with a lemon. Lemon ice cream, that is. This flavor was a passion and family favorite in all the generations, but especially the family patriarch, Deacon Spenser E. Morgan. Mr. Morgan absolutely loved Blue Bell Lemon ice cream and stocked up, with the flavor rotating in and out of season. Unfortunately, on October 6, 2017, Mr. Morgan passed away.

On July 13, 2018, I received a call from our visitor center that there was a family here celebrating the life of Mr. Morgan and requested that I come out and greet the family. As I walked out of the executive building, I immediately saw a sea of yellow shirts adorning our courtyard. The Morgan family, which consisted of sixteen brothers and sisters, had traveled from all over the country to celebrate the life of Mr. Morgan. No better way to celebrate than to travel to Brenham, Texas, and enjoy a scoop or two of his beloved Lemon ice cream while wearing shirts in the same shade of yellow.

To cap off the celebration, they collectively stood in front of the building and sang in beautiful harmony, their creation of "Weeee are Blue Bell People." It literally stopped people right in their tracks.

What an incredible tribute to a wonderful man and his passion for lemon ice cream, bringing them all together.

At Blue Bell, we receive numerous letters every day from consumers who love our products. This last letter, though, probably has impacted me more than any I have received, and truly reminded me that what we do every day, consistently, truly matters.

The letter came from a lady in Louisiana and was written on the same day her Pa passed away.

It reads ….

Dear Blue Bell Creameries Inc.,

I wanted to write you to share the memory of a special man with you—my grandpa, K.T. Phillips. Pa passed away this morning at 86 years young. He had a life-long passion for Blue Bell, and many of our family memories with Pa involve Blue Bell ice cream as well. Pa had a chest freezer he kept specifically for his Blue Bell. He would go to the store and buy a half gallon of every single Blue Bell flavor in stock – and he kept his freezer stocked at all times. Anytime anyone would visit Pa, you weren't leaving until you ate some Blue Bell—whether you wanted any or not! He would always offer, and even if you declined, he would disappear for about five minutes, and when he came back, he was carrying a bowl of ice cream—whatever flavor he thought you looked like you wanted that day—but Homemade Vanilla remained his favorite.

Over the past few years, Pa's mind was overtaken by Alzheimer's, but he remained faithful to Blue Bell. This past month, as Pa's mind and body deteriorated, he wouldn't eat or drink, and he couldn't remember his love for Blue Bell. But if we brought him some Homemade Vanilla ice cream, his blue eyes would sparkle as the flavors tickled his taste buds. And for just that moment we had our Pa back, and that is priceless.

Pa had seven children, seventeen grandchildren, and seventeen great-grandchildren and we all have fond memories of our Pa and Blue

Bell. I just wanted to share these memories so you will know that there are at least forty-one lives over here in Louisiana that have forever been impacted by your ice cream. For the remainder of our lives, we will eat Blue Bell and smile as we remember our Pa and how much he loved your ice cream—Thank you for that.

    Best Regards,

    Mandi

October 11/10

Blue Bell Creameries
Consumer Relations
P.O. Box 1807
Brenham, TX 77834

Dear Blue Bell Creameries Inc.,

I wanted to write to you to share the memory of a special man with you—my grandpa, K.T. Phillips. Pa passed away this morning at 86 years young. He had a life-long passion for Blue Bell and many of our family memories with Pa involve Blue Bell ice cream as well. Pa had a chest freezer he kept specifically for his Blue Bell. He would go to the store and buy a half gallon of every single Blue Bell flavor in stock—and he kept his freezer stocked at all times. Anytime anyone would visit Pa, you weren't leaving until you ate some Blue Bell—whether you wanted any or not! He would always offer and even if you declined, he would disappear for about five minutes and when he came back, he was carrying a bowl of ice cream—whatever flavor he thought you looked like you wanted that day—but Homemade Vanilla remained his favorite.

Over the past few years, Pa's mind was overtaken by Alzheimer's but he remained faithful to Blue Bell. This past month, as Pa's mind and body deteriorated, he wouldn't eat or drink—and he couldn't remember his love for Blue Bell—but if we brought him some Homemade Vanilla ice cream, his blue eyes would sparkle as the flavors tickled his taste buds. And for just that moment we had our Pa back, and that is priceless.

Pa had seven children, seventeen grandchildren, and seventeen great-grandchildren and we all have fond memories of our Pa and Blue Bell. I just wanted to share these memories so you will know that there are at least forty-one lives over here in Louisiana that have forever been impacted by your ice cream. For the remainder of our lives we will eat Blue Bell and smile as we remember our Pa and how much he loved your ice cream—thank you for that.

Best Regards,

Mandi S. Waites

Mandi S. Waites and the Phillips-Johnson Family

So often, we go through life day to day and wonder if what we do makes an impact. Each of the examples written in these chapters show that it's more than just ice cream, and it's how we approach each day that separates us from being just a brand in the freezer aisle of a supermarket, or the connecting piece that brings families together and takes you to a place that you can trust or feel safe.

As Christians, we also have a responsibility to how we live each day, unaware of the impact we might have on those around us. We should look different from the world because we have a reason to rise above the circumstances that we might find ourselves in. There are certain days when this can be very difficult, but remembering who you belong to can bridge the gap and provide that incredible peace. No matter where you work, what you do matters and can impact the kingdom for eternity.

13

Jenny Lake

I have always had a fascination with mountains and all their splendor. I'm not really sure why that is, especially since I grew up in San Antonio. The only true mountains I remember as a child came from either pictures or those I'd seen on TV or in the movies. Unless you count the "Hill Country," the closest mountain range from San Antonio is the Chisos Mountains, over 450 miles away. Don't get me wrong, the Hill Country is good, but you really can't count them as mountains. In the summer of my eighth-grade year, my personal and upfront views of true mountains dramatically changed.

Every summer, our youth group at church would take a choir mission trip to different parts of the country. It was a great way to share our faith and travel to places that were only in our dreams. The year before, I had crossed the threshold of going from elementary school to junior high, and even though I was still one of the youngest in the group I had made it into the big leagues as far as choir trips were concerned. That was my first mission trip. We traveled from San Antonio to Washington, D.C., and then up to New York City. I still remember almost everything from the Washington Monument to

New York's Times Square. But the most memorable event of the trip was the moment I asked the cutest seventh grader in our group to be my girlfriend on top of the Empire State Building. I took out of my pocket what I thought at the time was a beautiful ring. It had taken five attempts and as many quarters to retrieve the ring from a vending machine in the lobby below.

Despite my effort and the romantic setting, it was a hard NO on her part. What could have been the makings of an amazing *Sleepless in Seattle* story turned into one of my many failed attempts in the relationship department. Memorable, yes, but not the kind self-confidence is made of.

Fast-forward to the summer of 1972. That year our church staff put together a trip of a lifetime for any age, young or old. This amazing two-week journey took our group on a school bus through nine different states and included viewing landmark sites like Mount Rushmore, swimming in the Great Salt Lake, and ending with spectacular views of the Grand Canyon. As great as each of those places was to visit, what I remember most was Yellowstone National Park and the breathtaking Rocky Mountains.

Centered at the heart of those memories was my first view of the Grand Teton Mountain range. At first sight, I was mesmerized by their beauty, and I knew that one day, I would have to return and spend time taking in what I believe was some of God's finest work here on Earth. For someone who is afraid of heights, it was strange that the mountains seemed to draw me in as they did, yet their beauty filled me with more of a fear of respect and awareness than that of being afraid. I realize today that there are many other breathtaking mountain ranges all over the world, but the Grand Tetons were the first mountain range that left such a strong impression on me. I would also say that it erased all painful memories of the Empire State Building disaster from the year before.

Many years passed, but the desire to return one day still remained close to the top of my bucket list. There was something about the Grand Tetons that drew me in. In 2015, Anita and I decided that this was the year to check it off the list. We researched our journey and set our plans into motion to vacation in Jackson Hole, Wyoming. I would once again return to the Grand Tetons. She had never been to that part of the country, and I couldn't wait to experience it with her.

Unfortunately, 2015 was also the year our company's situation unfolded, and we had to put those plans on hold.

Fast-forward to 2021. After a few years of helping get Blue Bell back into the market and navigating through the Covid crisis, we were ready to get the bucket list back out and start checking boxes. In May, we retraced our steps, rebooked our trip, and off we went.

We both love to travel, and the itinerary included fly fishing in Idaho, checking to see if Old Faithful was still letting off steam, and plenty of hiking and bear-watching adventures, but our trip to Jenny Lake, which is set at the foothills of the Grand Teton Mountains, remained at the top of our list of the things to see and do while in Jackson Hole.

We completely blocked the entire day for our adventure, double-checking the weather forecast to make sure we had a trip of a lifetime. The locals had told us to be sure and get there early in order to get a parking spot. They also recommended we take the boat ride across Jenny Lake to hike up into the mountain on a journey that would take you to the beautiful "hidden falls." This amazing waterfall was carved into the mountain and was a must-see while hiking in the Tetons. I can't tell you how excited I was to take such a journey.

God's love for us includes so many breathtaking moments in our everyday lives, but unfortunately, we're too preoccupied to identify or recognize them due to the distractions the world throws at us. It's easy to see when your view is from the mountaintops, but there are so many hidden waterfalls all around us, we just have to watch for His glory in them to identify them, even in the simplest of situations.

My child, listen to what I say, and treasure my commands. Tune your ears to wisdom, and concentrate on understanding. Cry out for insight, and ask for understanding. Search for them as you would for silver; seek them like hidden treasures. Then you will understand what it means to fear the LORD, and you will gain knowledge of God.

—PROVERBS 2:1–5

Taking in the beauty of such a mountain range came naturally due to its size and stature, but the hidden treasure of a mighty waterfall took effort, determination, and wisdom. I was up for effort and determination, but as you will see, wisdom must have stayed in the cabin.

The day finally arrived, and we were up at the crack of dawn, rushing out to welcome the gorgeous sunrise that God had been up all night preparing. Beautiful crisp blue skies and fortyish degrees, we were pumped and ready for this amazing adventure. God didn't disappoint. We packed our survival equipment into our backpacks, including our camera, one can of bear spray, and two bottles of water, and took off.

Upon arrival, we realized that early for some wasn't necessarily early for others. The parking lot was basically empty, and we found a great place to park. With at least forty parking spots to accommodate guests of the park, only three were occupied. One apparently for the Park Ranger, since there were markings on the side of their jeep. Inhabited as it may have been, the beauty of the lake redirected our attention.

We casually walked down to the water and took a series of pictures, to include a few selfies and videos of "Ranger Rick" and his beautiful assistant, Anita. Over time, I developed a habit of making impromptu videos of the legendary character "Ranger Rick" when on vacation. At just the right moment, and only when in rare form, I would ad-lib a video of whatever came to mind or what we were up to, then send it back to the kids and grandkids at home, letting them know we were okay and corny as ever. I have since learned there really is a "Ranger Rick" trademarked and found in magazines, meaning I'll need to change to another fictitious name if I decide to attempt a second career with TikTok.

As we finished our photo shoot, we casually made our way to the boat launch. It wasn't long before we realized our promptness for a parking spot also meant our wait time would be up to two hours because the first boat ride of the day didn't leave until later that morning. We were too early! Even though we were motivated to get there before the other "tourists," the delay gave us the opportunity to re-strategize. There must be another way! Looking around, I was able to find that park ranger, and I asked if it was possible to walk to Hidden Falls.

Impatience mixed with excitement makes for a dangerous combination.

> **"Impatience mixed with excitement makes**
> **for a dangerous combination."**

This also seems consistent to my prayer life. Praying for God's direction is a daily request, but it seems like in no time, I jump in and take over, thinking I have a better way.

Now, I love park rangers and their love for the outdoors, but I have learned that anytime you ask anyone how far something is when hiking, you basically get the same answer: "It's not that far."

Her response of "not that far" was also consistent with my adventurous desire, but in the back of my mind, I wondered what could go wrong. My impatience, mixed with excitement, won my wife's approval. The ranger said, "It's only about two miles around the lake, and the trail will put you right on the path to Hidden Falls." We thought once we found the falls and spent time there, we could then take the boat ride back. It was a beautiful sunny day, with temperatures now in the lower fifties, and with her joint enthusiasm coming through, the decision became a no-brainer—so off we went. I could almost hear Forrest Gump's voice echoing the words, "I'm not a smart man, but I know what love is." As beautiful as Jenny Lake was, I would soon learn hiking around it wasn't the smartest of decisions.

The first part of the journey went as expected. The trail was obvious and well-marked. A few renegade hikers came up from behind us and moved on with ease and confidence, turning as they passed with final words of wisdom: "Watch out for bears." BEARS?

Fear has a way of disguising itself, then appearing out of nowhere. We had talked about bears but really didn't think they were much of a threat. We did have one can of bear spray and a whistle, but soon, self-doubt started to creep in, and I knew it wouldn't be the last.

After what seemed like a mile or so, the terrain started to take a turn for the worse in a variety of ways. The first sign of potential trouble was when we realized we had lost sight of the lake. We had been walking for some time without noticing the naturally made compass path had disappeared. The trail was evident, but our landmark, "Jenny Lake," was nowhere in sight. The next challenge on our journey came in the form of snow. Even though the temperature was in the fifties, the ground had become a mixture of mud and snow and then everything went totally white from the blanket that had been layered from the days before. It wasn't long before the trail became less obvious, and the snow became deeper.

I pulled out my phone to check my step monitor and realized we had already walked well past two miles. Unfortunately, there was no sign of the Hidden Falls anywhere in sight. Even so, we pressed forward. We were committed to getting to the falls, but I really began to worry. There was snow on the ground, no landmarks, and two water bottles that had already been opened. It's great to be adventurous, but not being properly prepared for such a journey allowed doubt and fear to live in my mind rent-free.

Periodically, we would pass other explorers coming back off the mountain, and they would repeatedly encourage us, using the same park ranger-prepared script, "You're almost there …" While we made our way in the snow, we began to hear what sounded like rushing water. The shot of adrenaline was short-lived when we realized it was the boat taking passengers across the lake! The very boat we were supposed to be on. As the leader of our two-person explorer team, I quickly reminded my wife of the fun we were having and how this was strengthening our marriage. Sometimes, it's best to stay quiet, and this was one of those times. If ever there was a time to hit the easy button to remedy the situation, this was the time.

Just when I thought things couldn't get any worse, I heard Anita scream. When I looked back, her right leg had disappeared into the snow almost all the way to her waist. It was obvious we were not on the trail, and not knowing where to plant our next step became the newest challenge of our Dickson and Dickson expedition. After 16,784 steps, two empty water bottles, one prepared can of bear spray, and two exhausted hikers, we came across a sign that said, "Hidden Falls to the left and Boat dock to the right."

We both froze in our tracks, yet were too afraid to make eye contact. We had reached a new critical decision point, and this time, I wasn't about to lead off with a recommendation. I was supportive of either choice. The competitive part of me said, finish the journey, yet my body ached as it reminded me how out of shape I had become. Finally, looking at Anita, I received nonverbal advice to finish the race. "We have come too far to bail out now." Cramping legs and all, I knew she was right and to the left we went. It wasn't long before we could hear the sound of rushing water, then joined the newly formed group of tourists that had arrived by boat.

As beautiful as the Hidden Falls were, it was the challenges of the journey that will forever be etched in my mind. That adventurous day is such a reflection of our lives. We start out on a new marriage or maybe a new job with sky's-the-limit enthusiasm, yet at some point, life has a way of changing our path at the most unexpected times.

I can't help thinking about the lives of Jesus's disciples. They were all personally called by Christ to follow Him. And they did, immediately. His dream team may have looked rough on the outside—full of tax collectors and fishermen—but Jesus knew their hearts. Hearing His voice, they recognized He was the one they had been waiting for, even though they really didn't know or understand what that meant.

Even though they really didn't understand what they were signing up for, they believed He was the Messiah, Savior of the world, and they had front-row seats to see it unfold in a way our human minds could only dream of. Yet with each miracle Jesus performed, their faith meter was restored, only to lose signal again when trials came back their way. Sound familiar?

To illustrate further, we catch up to Jesus in Mark 6:30–44. The apostles have just returned from their mission trip assignment, and

Jesus suggests they go off to a quiet place to rest for a while. Even though their trip had been successful, Jesus recognized many people were around the area, and they hadn't had the opportunity to eat and rest. They also were still mourning the death of John the Baptist, who was killed while they were gone.

But as they got into their boat, they were spotted by many people on the shore who were eager to meet Jesus. The word was out. Jesus was there, and suddenly a multitude of people gathered.

The crowd was hoping for more than just a sighting. Many were running in desperation like lost sheep without a shepherd. Some were possibly praying for a miracle, others may have been hoping for a king, and others simply didn't want to miss out on what would surely be the talk of the town—Jesus's arrival was big news!

We catch up in verse 35 …

> *35 Late in the afternoon, his disciples came to Him and said, "This is a remote place, and it's already getting late. 36 Send the crowds away so they can go to the nearby farms and villages and buy something to eat."*
>
> *37 But Jesus said, "You feed them."*
>
> *"With what?" they asked. "We'd have to work for months to earn enough money[a] to buy food for all these people!"*
>
> *38 "How much bread do you have?" He asked. "Go and find out."*
>
> *They came back and reported, "We have five loaves of bread and two fish."*
>
> *39 Then Jesus told the disciples to have the people sit down in groups on the green grass. 40 So they sat down in groups of fifty or a hundred.*

41 Jesus took the five loaves and two fish, looked up toward Heaven, and blessed them. Then, breaking the loaves into pieces, he kept giving the bread to the disciples so they could distribute it to the people. He also divided the fish for everyone to share. 42 They all ate as much as they wanted, 43 and afterward, the disciples picked up twelve baskets of leftover bread and fish. 44 A total of 5,000 men and their families were fed.[b]

The disciples had already seen Jesus calm the storms but taking a few fish and a couple of loaves of bread, and feeding the masses didn't seem to impress them. Maybe they were frustrated that the crowds had taken Jesus away from their "alone" time. They may have forgotten Jesus's abilities to control nature or, in this case, feed the sheep—His sheep—by multiplying the offering of five loaves and two fishes. Either way, they missed it.

Similarly, we seem to identify God's artistic ability in a beautiful sunrise or unexplainable mountaintop experience, but when we get consumed in our struggles, we often first lose sight of Him and become consumed with the struggle instead of the Savior.

As soon as the multitudes are fed, Jesus insists the disciples get back in the boat and head out across the lake while he stays behind to be alone and pray. Similar to the encounter in Chapter 4, the winds pick up, and the waves become unbearable. From the shore, Jesus sees the struggle and walks out to them.

Mark 6: 45–50

45 Immediately after this, Jesus insisted that his disciples get back into the boat and head across the lake to Bethsaida, while He sent the people home. ⁴⁶After telling everyone goodbye, He went up into the hills by Himself to pray.

⁴⁷ Late that night, the disciples were in their boat in the middle of the lake, and Jesus was alone on land. ⁴⁸ He saw that they were in serious trouble, rowing hard and struggling against the wind and waves. About three o'clock in the morning[a] Jesus came toward them, walking on the water. He intended to go past them, ⁴⁹ but when they saw Him walking on the water, they cried out in terror, thinking He was a ghost. ⁵⁰ They were all terrified when they saw him.

But Jesus spoke to them at once. "Don't be afraid," he said. "Take courage! I am here![b]"

The disciples find themselves right back in a storm, coming off a successful mission trip and a miraculous "all-you-could-eat" fish and bread dinner, but they had lost sight of Jesus, even though Jesus hadn't lost sight of them. Don't get me wrong, storms can do that, and yes, screaming in terror is as real as it gets, yet the more you are prepared for the waves, the easier it is to recognize Jesus standing in the middle of the storm. Jesus, as only Jesus can do, calmly says, "It's alright. I am here. Don't be afraid." For Peter, though, that's not enough proof.

Matthew explains this account even further when he writes about Peter's raw emotions when he hears Jesus say those words.

²⁷ But Jesus spoke to them at once. "Don't be afraid," he said. "Take courage. I am here![a]"

²⁸ Then Peter called to him, "Lord, if it's really you, tell me to come to you, walking on the water."

²⁹ "Yes, come," Jesus said.

So Peter went over the side of the boat and walked on the water toward Jesus. [30] *But when he saw the strong[b] wind and the waves, he was terrified and began to sink. "Save me, Lord!" he shouted.*

[31] *Jesus immediately reached out and grabbed him. "You have so little faith," Jesus said. "Why did you doubt me?"*

[32] *When they climbed back into the boat, the wind stopped.*

—MATTHEW 14: 27 - 32

It was one thing for the disciples to have fear when all seemed lost on their first storm-riddled ride—even with Jesus on the boat. But to go at it alone, without the Savior in sight, meant their measurement of faith would have to be multiplied. Whether Jesus is on the boat, standing on the water, or even watching from the shore, He is with you. So instead of turning down life's next boat ride, drop fear like an anchor and either curl up next to Him and rest or step out of the boat in faith. The key is simple: Don't take your eyes off the one that speaks the words, "Take courage; I am here."

The key is simple: Don't take your eyes off the one who says, "Take courage; I am here."

What Peter focused on became his reality, and when his focus changed, he began to sink. In the same way, what we focus on becomes our reality. We must stay focused on Jesus, no matter how high the waves seem to be.

The boat ride back across Jenny Lake allowed me to reflect on the day's long journey, realizing that as much as I think I am in control, I am not! Praise God that there is a Savior who loves me, and even though

I know "I'm not a smart man ... I know what love is." It's a thing called grace. Something I received from both my wife and my Savior that day.

14

Finishing Strong

Ever since I was young, I absolutely loved watching the Summer Olympics. Don't get me wrong, I love the winter games too, but there was something special about the summer games. Especially track and field. Now, maybe this is because track was the only real sport I could compete in as a six-foot, 130-pound athlete (and I use the word athlete very loosely). There was also something special about amateur athletes (at that time) coming together from all over the world, to compete on the world stage to see who was the fastest, strongest, or most skilled at their individual sport.

In some cases, the event took hours, like the marathon, but other events, like the 100- or 200-meter dash, were over within seconds, leaving no room for error. The athletes were the best of the best, and they had committed their lives to earn the right to carry that title. In most cases, the difference between success or failure was decided in as little as a hundredth (if not a thousandth) of a second, separating the gold, silver, or bronze medal from a four-year wait until the next attempt. You had to be on, and you had to be ready.

Even though a majority of the events in the Olympics are for individuals, there are also certain team events that are equally exciting. Who could ever forget the ending of the 1972 Olympic men's basketball final that is still regarded as one of the most controversial events in Olympic history. With a series of questionable interpretations of the rules by the referees, seconds were added back on the clock, giving the Soviet Union the opportunity to defeat the United States by one point, marking the first loss by the United States ever in the event.

Moving from the basketball court to track and field, one of the most exciting events for me was watching the 4 x 100 relay race. Not only do you have to put together four of the fastest human beings from your country to run one of the four legs of the race, but they must also pass a baton from one to another within a specific area of their lane in order to officially complete the race. Speed, concentration, and finesse are the three key ingredients for success, and it all takes place in less than forty seconds.

One of my more recent memories of this event took place during the 2008 Summer Olympic Games, held in Beijing National Stadium in Beijing, China. That year, over 2,000 athletes came from 200 nations to compete on this world stage once again. Team USA had established itself as one of the favorites in sprint relays, setting many Olympic records in past years, including the most recent record of 37.40 seconds at the 1992 Barcelona Olympics. Once again, the USA team, composed of Rodney Martin, Travis Padgett, Darvis Patton, and Tyson Gay, were center stage and were expected to threaten the Olympic record with their speed and agility. In their qualifying heat, Team USA was positioned in lane seven, right next to their strongest challenger, the team of Trinidad and Tobago. For Team USA, the gold medal was theirs to lose, and if they ran it with perfection, another world record would be theirs to cherish.

On the afternoon of August 21ˢᵗ, Beijing experienced intermittent showers throughout the warm day, making track conditions less favorable. Equal, though, for everyone. The goal was to qualify for the finals to be run the next day. The race started with perfection as Rodney Martin exploded like a rocket out of the starting blocks and sprinted around the first curve with ease, then handed the baton off to Travis Padgett. Down the backstretch, Padgett seemed to widen the USA lead, setting the stage for the next handoff, which went flawlessly, to David Patton. As Patton came around the final curve, it was apparent that Team USA was in the lead with one exchange of the baton to go and the finish line to celebrate. Unfortunately, and to the crowd's disbelief, that one handoff never happened.

As Tyson Gay reached back to receive the baton, the aluminum feel of the baton never hit his hand. Patton's first attempt failed to connect, and the second found him tossing it in desperation to an unknowing Gay. Gay never received the baton that night, nor did he get to run the final anchor leg for his American team. His hopes for a gold medal and possibly a world record came crashing down on the surface of the damp track that night, to the disappointment of his team and all Americans. Just a fraction of a second, or the slight miscalculation of an orchestrated hand off, separates those who make the record books from all the others that try but come up short.

On the other hand, the lesson that can be learned from each experience prepares you for the next opportunity. I heard Michael Jordan once say, "I've missed more than 9000 shots in my career. I've lost almost 300 games. Twenty-six times, I've been trusted to take the game-winning shot and missed. I've failed over and over and over again in my life. And that is why I succeed."

Ultimately, it comes down to doing one's best every day, consistently, that puts them in the arena to begin with. As powerful and exuberating as victory can be, it's usually the struggles in the journey that define you. Even amid such a major letdown as described, we are always given a choice in how we respond. We can either camp out and allow defeat to become a permanent resident, or pivot from the experience and learn from the lessons that are being taught. In doing so, with determination, you can come back even stronger. The key is to stay true to who you are and not compromise.

At Blue Bell, from the time the fresh milk and cream arrive at our manufacturing plants to when all the ingredients are combined, frozen, and delivered to each store, every step is critical to achieving ultimate success: the freshest-tasting ice cream possible. If, anywhere along the way, the baton is dropped, it affects the overall outcome.

A NUTTY DILEMMA

As a company, we are constantly faced with decisions that not only affect the bottom line, but also the consumers, employees, and shareholders alike. As described in earlier chapters, there are a variety of ways to label ice cream, with the percent of butterfat (no less than 10 percent) and air (or overrun) no more than 100 percent, as the only two mandatory standards of identity. As long as these two principles are met, ice cream can be altered to meet internal standards or expectations. Compromising through expectations will lead to inconsistency.

In the late eighties and early nineties, Blue Bell was faced with a very difficult decision. The problem was centered around the price of pecans and how it affected the profitability of one of our top-selling flavors, Buttered Pecan. This flavor was a uniquely rich, buttered pecan ice cream with lightly salted, roasted pecan halves. It had grown in popularity and was a mainstay in our year-round lineup. Due to unfavorable weather conditions, the pecan crop during some of those years was slim at best, raising the cost of pecans per pound to unprecedented prices.

The dilemma for the company was one of the following: 1) Do we continue to make Buttered Pecan, but raise the price of each half gallon and pint for just that flavor? 2) Do we cut back on the number of pecans we put into each carton and keep the product at the same price? Or, 3) Do we discontinue making Buttered Pecan altogether until the price of pecans drops? In early discussions, management made the decision that the second option was unacceptable. Changing the amount of pecans added would be an easy fix, but it would be the first step in compromising who we are as a company. It's easy to cut back the amount by just a little, but once you start down that path, it's not long before you make a product with just a few pecans or pecan meal or even worse, a product without any pecans at all. This was unacceptable and would not be considered. Not to over-sell our Buttered Pecan, but next time you enjoy a scoop, look for the amazing number of pecans in every carton and, hopefully, every bite, and then imagine if they weren't there at all. We'd have to change the name from Buttered Pecan to Buttered Pecan't. Sorry … Okay, that was pretty bad.

We decided to discontinue the flavor altogether, but due to the tremendous demand, we eventually brought it back. We ended up changing the packaging and raised the price accordingly. The situation became such a point of topic that the *Dallas Morning News* even ran a feature story with the headline that read something like, "If You Were CEO of Blue Bell, What Would You Do?" The beauty of this example was that we refused to compromise on the expectation and popularity of this flavor, and that philosophy remains consistent to this day.

There is a solid line in supply chain ethics when determining right from wrong, and one's moral compass as a leader can define and affect your whole organization. Merriam-Webster defines supply chain as:

"The chain of processes, businesses, etc. by which a commodity is produced and distributed: the companies, materials, and systems involved in manufacturing and delivering goods."

Combine that definition with ethics, and you have a definition that would include a cultural tradition and responsibility to produce a product or provide a service that treats both the employees and the environment ethically.

As Christians, we, too, are faced with this situation on a daily basis, and it boils down to how we treat our fellow man. A good self-examination would be to look at your prayer life. The motive of what you pray for will determine the motive of your heart.

> **"The motive of what you pray for will
> determine the motive of your heart."**

In Matthew, when Jesus was confronted about which of the commandments was the most important, Jesus replied:

*37 Jesus replied, "'You must **love the Lord your God** with all your heart, all your soul, and all your mind.' 38 This is the first and greatest commandment. 39 A second is equally important: 'Love your neighbor as yourself.' 40 The entire law and all the demands of the prophets are based on these two commandments."*

—MATTHEW 22:37–40

As we live our lives day to day, we might be the only example of "Jesus" that someone might see. If we claim the name of Christ as our Savior and yet live our lives in a way that doesn't reflect His love, we drop the baton! If we are to love each other as ourselves, what does that say about ourselves? The problem comes back to the battle within and determining when, where, and what we compromise. Dying to self, daily, hour by hour, and minute by minute was the example we see in the life of Jesus when He walked on this Earth. Focusing on completing the race should be our goal for as long as we are able.

Yes, unfortunately, we will drop the baton numerous times, but unlike the race mentioned, there's a thing called grace, and through His forgiveness, Jesus reaches down, picks up the baton, and says, "Try again!" He's not asking for perfection; He's asking for your heart. And in the same way, in the darkest of times, when things don't make sense, and you can't feel His hand, trust His heart! He loves you more than you will ever comprehend, and this child-like faith will allow you to rest in His arms. When you and I realize the power that comes from this devotion, peace will flow like a mighty river and take you to the finish line, where the gold will cover the streets.

> *¹ And let us run with endurance the race God has set before us. ² We do this by keeping our eyes on* **Jesus**, *the champion who initiates and perfects our faith. Because of the joy awaiting him, he endured the cross, disregarding its shame. Now he is seated in the place of honor beside God's throne.*

—HEBREWS 12: 1-2

15

Tonya

It was the last workday of the last full week in 2018. There is nothing like week fifty-two. Bringing another year to an end, with exciting expectations right around the corner, right after the final round of "Auld Lang Syne." Our main office staff was putting the closing touches on the weekly paperwork procedures while end-of-year inventories were being totaled and documented. The few die-hard employees that remained were holding down the creamery while many of us were gearing up for the second half of the Christmas and New Year celebrations to include a full day or two of college football.

Our company had been through a lot in the past few years, and there was no doubt that we had truly been blessed with a second chance from the listeria events that took place in 2015, but sometimes God's continued blessing comes at the most unexpected times and in the most unexpected ways.

The phone call came in around 4:30 p.m. in the afternoon. Up until then, the switchboard had been relatively quiet, apart from a few last-minute salesmen trying to reach their annual quotas or consumers looking for a holiday favorite flavor.

Tallie Tootle, my administrative assistant, took the call, praying the request would be a simple one. She had no idea at the time how this very special call would impact her. The voice on the other end identified herself as Jennifer Barkley. A name unfamiliar to Tallie, yet immediately she could tell by the tone of Jennifer's voice that she seemed frantic. Jennifer explained that her sister, Tonya Nuckolls, had been battling cancer, and they didn't expect her to make it through the weekend. Her call was centered around a specific request, and she was desperate for Tallie's help.

I once heard it said that "when fear knocks at your door, it has a way of grabbing your attention" and Jennifer's desperation demanded Tallie's fullest attention. According to Jennifer, Tonya's cancer had taken an aggressive, strong turn for the worse. Time was no longer a friend here on Earth, yet eternity was on the other side and waiting with open arms. Before that glorious moment, Tonya had two important wishes.

Her first wish was to live long enough to celebrate her fifty-ninth birthday—which was in three days. It also seemed like a reasonable goal before her health rapidly declined. For Tonya, though, they had been fifty-nine great years, and she was ready to enter Heaven.

Tonya's second wish was to serve Blue Bell ice cream at her memorial service.

What Jennifer didn't know at the time was that she had connected to one of the most compassionate individuals I have ever worked with at Blue Bell. Tallie truly has a heart of gold, and helping others comes naturally, regardless of what day it might be. When others might apologetically dismiss the request, Tallie went into action.

With only thirty minutes to spare before the clock struck 5:00 p.m. and our business would close for the holiday, Tallie realized she'd have to attempt to make the impossible possible.

Tallie's first task was to get Tonya's location from Jennifer. Once identifying southern Alabama as the area, Tallie notified our local branch manager David Brownlow, who managed our Mobile, Alabama branch. Tallie explained the situation and Jennifer's request to purchase two hundred Homemade Vanilla cups for a memorial–while praying for the best yet preparing for the worst. Hearing the urgency in Tallie's voice, David was eager to help and asked for Jennifer's contact information.

To connect the two, Tallie sent the following e-mail to both:

Hi there!

Jennifer, meet David - David, meet Jennifer.

Jennifer - David Brownlow is the Branch Manager at our Mobile location and will be the one you can contact regarding everything. (The branch phone number and email address were shared).

David - Jennifer's sister has the end stages of cancer and will more likely pass away pretty soon. Her 59th birthday is on New Year's Eve, and they're hoping she's able to celebrate it. Her favorite flavor is Homemade Vanilla, and it's her wish for everyone attending her celebration of life service to "share" a cup of it. Jennifer is trying to get a more accurate head count but is expecting around 200 people for the service. Jennifer's last name is Barkley. (Her phone number and email were shared.)

I'm going to let you guys take it from here. Please let me know if I can help with anything.

Jennifer - I know you have a lot going on, but if you would reach out and let me know the details of the service (when you have them), I know our president would like to send you something. I can't imagine what you're going through right now, but I wish you the best.

David - thank you for everything.

Take care,

Tallie

David followed up this email with a call to Jennifer and assured her that he could be reached at any time and would be ready in the event Tonya's condition took a turn for the worst.

Once Jennifer was comforted with this news, she also remembered the second half of her sister's special ice cream request. In the midst of all her "thank yous" to David on the phone, she asked if it would be possible to also get the Blue Bell wooden spoons to go with the cups. Individually wrapped wooden spoons were made available to accounts (like schools or convenient stores) that sold single-serve ice cream cups for immediate consumption.

Even though David assumed the need for the spoons was simply to enjoy the ice cream, he didn't fully understand the reason it was so important to Jennifer. He said he would make it happen. It wasn't until the following week that we all learned that both of Tonya's prayer requests had been answered.

On December 31st, Tonya celebrated her fifty-ninth birthday with a small gathering of her family and friends. A milestone indeed, especially in her condition.

She was also told the news about the soon-to-be celebration of life in her honor and how it would include Blue Bell Homemade Vanilla. Even though her body was frail, her mind was still sharp, and she cried tears of joy.

On Sunday, January 6, 2019, at 11:00 p.m., Tonya stepped into Heaven to meet her Savior.

On Wednesday, January 9th, Tonya's family and friends celebrated her entrance into the Kingdom of Heaven while enjoying the ice cream that she loved on Earth. Even in the smallest of details of our lives, we find God's faithfulness.

Two days before the celebration, Jennifer sent another email to Tallie; this time, we understood the significance of the request. Her email read:

From: Jennifer Barkley
Sent: Monday, January 07, 2019 2:00 PM
To: Tallie Tootle
Subject: Tonya Nuckolls Funeral Arrangements

I cannot tell you how much we, as her family, appreciate what you and David have done for us in her memory. I was able to tell Tonya while her mind was still sharp, and she cried. I wish I knew how many times the story has already been told, from my phone call to you to the final result. Tonya wanted a scripture written on the spoons and I had them printed. It reads as follows: **Oh, taste and see that the Lord is good. Psalm 34:8**

So now you can see how this memory of her will not only be a testimony of the kindness of Blue Bell, or her life, but also a testimony of how God cares about the smallest details of our lives. And THAT is what Tonya would have wanted. So we thank you again for all you have done.

Blessings,
Jennifer Barkley

After returning from vacation, Tallie shared this amazing story with me and the impact it had had on her during the holiday season. But as moving as Tonya's story had become, God wasn't finished … in fact, the story was just getting started. I was extremely moved by Tonya's impact here on Earth and how everything came together at the last minute, but ultimately, Tonya's wish was that God would receive all the glory.

During our annual sales and production meeting held just weeks later, I shared Tonya's story, emphasizing that what we do each day truly matters. I stressed that our work is so much more than just making and selling ice cream—it's creating memories and touching lives. Ice cream can be enjoyed in the best of times or served to comfort during the worst of times. For Tonya, Homemade Vanilla brought comfort during life's final moments, but even more importantly, she recognized where the blessing came from. It was through the goodness of our Lord throughout her life.

In the following weeks, Tallie couldn't get Tonya off her mind. The experience had impacted her deeply. So, she reached out to Jennifer one last time.

She wrote:

Hi Jennifer,

I wanted to reach out to you not only to see how you're doing but to also say "thank you." I know you believed we did something for you and your sister, but you don't realize the gift you gave us. At the beginning of each year, we hold our annual sales meeting where management from all our branches come together to start the year out with "a bang." Our president usually tells a story about how something as simple as our ice cream can make a difference in people's lives. We're blessed to have many wonderful experiences with our customers, but your story was the one he chose to share. There wasn't a dry eye in the room and knowing she associated our ice cream with such a beautiful scripture was something none of us will forget. He truly had a difficult time, even "getting through" telling the story.

I know there will never be a day that you won't miss your sister, but I hope you know that without meeting or even talking to her, she made a difference in OUR lives as well.

Thank you again,

Take care,
~ Tallie

Time passed and it wasn't until later that summer when Jennifer reached back out to Tallie to update her on Tonya's story. She wrote:

Tallie:

I apologize for the amount of time it has taken me to respond, but I was absolutely overcome when I read your email. I was just amazed at how Tonya's story had touched many lives even there at Blue Bell and throughout the company.

I wrote a public post on Facebook about it and how God can use something as trivial as your favorite ice cream to reach others for His glory and the ripple effect that takes place. I was so happy to tell her 20-year-old son, Christopher, about it. I wanted him to understand that there was a reason and God's perfect timing in her death. And he was so touched.

People began commenting and sharing the story until it now has touched 17,000 lives in 46 US states and at least 14 countries the last time I checked. I can only assume it has not reached all 50 states because it is not sold in those states. (Bless their hearts.)

As humbled as I was at the generosity of your company, I am discovering through the comments that it is a routine thing for Blue Bell. The people of Texas are especially proud of their state and the fact that you are based there. There are so many comments about how good the company is and of course how they love your ice cream. Many have even stated they will switch to BB and will always remember this story.

The ripple effect is far greater when God is involved. I believe everyone involved in this story will receive many blessings for years to come because of it. Please pass on my gratitude to your president. I am forever grateful for the generosity and sincerity of your company in our time of loss.

Jennifer later shared this wonderful story on her Facebook page:

August 9 at 5:28 AM

It has been a while since I posted anything but I need to share this story regarding my sister who went home to be with Jesus this past January. Tonya Willams Nuckolls LOVED Blue Bell ice cream. We, the family, would always give her grief about eating it because she was diabetic. Two years prior to her passing as she was planning the inevitable, she declared that she wanted every guest at the funeral to have a cup of Blue Bell ice cream with a scripture on it. And she made me promise her that it would happen.

When the time came near, I wondered where I could get 200 cups of Blue Bell ice cream with only a couple of days' notice. I googled Blue Bell headquarters and "happened" to get the executive assistant to the CEO and president of Blue Bell. After she expressed her sympathies and asked a few questions about Tonya and her favorite flavor, she told me how to go about picking up the ice cream that Blue Bell would be donating on her behalf. I was able to share the outcome of the phone call with Tonya and she smiled. But she could never have known the impact she was about to truly make.

We were blown away by the kindness the company had shown, but it was the email I received yesterday that made me reflect and put everything into perspective. You may read it in the pic below.

I knew, as did all those around her, how Tonya personally touched many people in her lifetime. But she literally pointed hundreds of people-across the country to Jesus by her one decision. I tell you this not to brag on her or the company involved but to show you how God can align every tiny detail of our lives to point back to His greatness and goodness. He loves you so much and He wants to give you every opportunity to get to know Him personally and intimately and will even use unconventional ways to do so. We can not even imagine the ripple effect of our everyday decisions on the Kingdom of God.

"Oh, taste and see that the Lord is good."

Psalm 38:4

#bluebell

This story is such a great reminder that everything we say, or, even more importantly, every action we take, can have a positive or negative impact on the Kingdom of God. I once heard it said, "We should always be witnessing for the kingdom, and if you have to, use words."

Jennifer's phone call to Tallie could have gone unanswered or just ignored, but the heart of the faithful said otherwise. I truly believe God's message came through at such a critical time and for His glory. Ice cream, in this case, happened to be the catalyst that connected those two to the love of Christ, and eventually, it was Jennifer's faithfulness and determination that made it possible to share the love of Christ that Tonya so desperately wanted.

Oh, taste and see that the Lord is good.

—PSALM 38:4

16

Choice

One of the more popular questions I get asked is: "How many different flavors of ice cream do you make each year?" The number can range anywhere from forty to forty-five, but surprisingly, there are often times we have omitted someone's favorite, forcing them to choose from the remaining selection. On the bright side, they get to choose a different flavor and, hopefully, they will find a new creation they can call their own.

Whether or not we admit it, we like to make our own choices. We may say we don't care when asked, "Where do you want to go eat?" but honestly, we have an opinion. With practically everything we do from the time we get up to when we go to bed, we make choices. It is part of God's beautiful design, and yet, so often, our decisions lead us down a path that takes divine intervention to recover from.

By definition, the word "choice," in its simplicity, is the act of choosing. (Sometimes Webster makes things easy for us). As stated earlier in this book, from the beginning of mankind, the ability to choose was a gift, and it became a permanent resident, cemented deep within the core of us all.

In just six days, God created this most amazing earth for all of mankind to enjoy. Obviously, something only the Creator of the universe could do. From the most amazing variety of fish and animals to majestic mountain ranges, lush green pastures, and ocean fronts, every detail was crafted into motion. If there are any still that doubt, just take in one of God's signature sunrises or sunsets, but be careful: They can take one's breath away. It just doesn't get any better. To think Adam and Eve had these indescribable surroundings all to themselves and the gift of choice ultimately tied like a bow on each of the two trees in the garden. If they choose wisely their lives and everything around them would be as God originally planned for in His creation, but knowledge is a powerful thing.

With all the choices they were confronted with throughout the day, their ultimate choice came down to their love and devotion to God Himself. Through His plan, He gave them the freedom or option in turn to love Him. There was no artificial intelligence programming here. They were God's creation, and every decision that Adam and Eve made, whether it was right or wrong, came with a consequence. I can almost hear Adam saying, "Do I work the garden today, or maybe it can wait until tomorrow?" Or when discussing lunch with Eve, "Which fruit looks good today, the oranges or maybe the grapes, or maybe we should have both?" Boy, they sure made a … *pear*!

Having this freedom of choice is in our DNA. Laws were created to keep us in line, but many claim they have the right to do otherwise. Again, with each decision, there is a consequence, good or bad, and fortunately, God is right there to guide us if we let Him. Yogi Berra, the famous New York Yankees catcher and coach, said it best: "When you come to the fork in the road, take it," and that's what we do each and every day. That's by design, and that's how God created the world to be.

Because the greatest decision of all decisions ever made was centered around two trees, and the desire of "knowledge" was chosen over "life," the tree of life was removed not only from the garden, but from Earth altogether. From that moment on, knowledge kicked in, and with it came this thing called sin. We seldom consider the fact that, every moment of our life, we stand in front of that very same tree, desiring knowledge, and are ironically given the same freedom to choose. When we realize we have made a bad decision, we seem to claim, "The devil made me do it," but often, it's our selfish desires that overpower what was the right choice.

From birth, this gift of knowledge immediately became our best friend or worst enemy, depending on which decision was made. Unfortunately, we also learn that our nature is centered inwardly and not upwardly. Selfishness arrives the moment we are born and immediately announces to the world who's in control. Ask a tired parent who's been up all night with a screaming baby who's selfish, and who's selfless. It's in our nature and comes naturally.

Our decisions are then woven together to create the world in which we live, leaving all its effects and consequences as our legacy in history. I cannot begin to explain why bad things happen to good people, or why hatred seems to dominate our world so much today, other than that, through a series of choices, good and bad things happen. Again, the gift of knowledge also opened the door for evil to take up residence through this thing called sin. I'm not talking about trying to be good or initially making bad choices; I'm talking about decisions that are made in the absence of God in the process.

Even Satan knew this when tempting Eve in the garden.

⁴ *"You won't die!" the serpent replied to the woman.* ⁵ *"God knows*

that your eyes will be opened as soon as you eat it, and you will be like God, knowing both good and evil."

—GENESIS 3:4-5

Pretty convincing, even though I wonder if they really understood the difference between good and evil. Either way, being "like God" meant they no longer would need Him. Or so they thought ...

So, how do we navigate through each and every day with this so-called gift of choice? Well, it first starts with what is the greatest decision that we can possibly make—choosing to accept the gift of eternal life of Jesus Christ as your personal savior. By doing so, we are immediately transformed into a new creation, made in Christ! His desires become our desires. Yet when we fail, every decision made that comes from our sinful nature has been nailed up on another tree, the cross on which Christ died. Both the sins of our past and those in the future. What an amazing gift indeed.

[17] This means that anyone who belongs to Christ has become a new person. The old life is gone; a new life has begun!

[18] And all of this is a gift from God, who brought us back to himself through Christ. And God has given us this task of reconciling people to him.

—2 CORINTHIANS 5: 17-18

Ultimately, we will pass from life here on Earth, but our earthly death will not be the last stop on our journey. Depending on the personal choice we make by accepting or rejecting Christ, eternity will be spent with Him or without Him. The absence of Christ then leaves you in total darkness.

I heard it once said that darkness is the complete absence of light, but we can't study darkness on its own. Darkness occurs when light isn't present. If Christ is the light of the world, without His presence, one would be in total darkness. Similarly, evil is the absence of God in people's hearts and the lack of love and faith in Him. Love and faith are like light; the absence is what leads to evil. Death is certain, and like our choices, when it comes, it comes with a consequence. But instead of darkness, we will forever live in His light!

I love the way 1 Corinthians 15:54–58 describes this:

54 Then, when our dying bodies have been transformed into bodies that will never die, this Scripture will be fulfilled:

"Death is swallowed up in victory.

55 O death, where is your victory?

O death, where is your sting?"

56 For sin is the sting that results in death, and the law gives sin its power. 57 But thank God! He gives us victory over sin and death through our Lord Jesus Christ.

58 So, my dear brothers and sisters, be strong and immovable. Always work enthusiastically for the Lord, for you know that nothing you do for the Lord is ever useless.

Having the assurance of eternal life is a tremendous gift, but while here on Earth, life can still become extremely difficult. You can count on it. As much as I don't understand the trials in my life, as a child of God, I have tried desperately hard to embrace those moments. Especially when things just don't make sense. It's in the fire that I know I am being refined and "trust" becomes my closest companion. Sometimes, though, I try to claim it, but I question whether I really believe it.

A great example of this is found in Mark 8: 27–29:

> *27 Jesus and his disciples left Galilee and went up to the villages near Caesarea Philippi. As they were walking along, he asked them, "Who do people say I am?"*
>
> *28 "Well," they replied, "some say John the Baptist, some say Elijah, and others say you are one of the other prophets."*
>
> *29 Then he asked them, "But who do you say I am?"*
>
> *Peter replied, "You are the Messiah."*

Believing Jesus is the Messiah is my anchor, and I am so thankful that He is patient in times when trust becomes the hardest thing I can do. Turning fear into peace can be a daily battle, but He is there to hold your hand and guide you through.

> *2 Dear brothers and sisters, when troubles of any kind come your way, consider it an opportunity for great joy. 3 For you know that when your faith is tested, your endurance has a chance to grow.*
>
> —JAMES 1: 2–3

So, how do we journey through? We can seek comfort through scripture or godly teaching, but simply praying can change the world. The only way to hear the voice of God is through communication, and the power of prayer can move mountains. There are countless stories in the Bible where God listened to the prayers of His people then answered them—even prayers that take certain individuals down a road they would have rather not gone down.

When storms come into our lives, we must remember to step in the footprints that God has laid before us. Go to the front of the boat and sleep next to the one that calms the seas, or better yet, step out on the water and focus on the face of the savior. No life jacket is required! Just hold His hand.

Come before God as you are, not clothed in worldly expectations, and trust, trust, trust. In those moments of fear, allow peace to take over. Find your second wind, and finish the race stronger than ever. God so desperately wants a personal relationship with you and welcomes you just as you are. Come and embrace Him with open arms, come to Him wherever you are. Close your eyes and be consumed by His light, and as close as the sound of a soft whisper, you will see Him everywhere.

In my life there have been many forks in the road where I had to rely on the Holy Spirit for direction and guidance. From leaning into new and exciting positions at Blue Bell to traversing mountains with my wife to tackling the monster slide—my life has been filled with moments where I had to trust in the Lord's plan for my life.

What started as a simple college assignment turned into forty-three years of working at Blue Bell. I'm writing these words as I prepare for retirement and begin a new chapter. As long as I have the baton in my hand and His scripture in my heart, I will continue to run the race, stepping where the Father leads and focusing on His light for direction.

Life can be an amazing journey, filled with highs and lows, but I must remember to approach every day...

One Scoop at a Time!

Acknowledgments

I have to start by thanking Mark Batterson and his inspirational book, *Chase the Lion*. The challenging subtitle, "If your dream doesn't scare you, it's too small" set into motion a passion deep within me to one day write a book. His books and his friendship have continued to motivate and inspire me to chase after this dream. Thank you so much Mark for your noncompromising faith and for believing in this journey.

To my Blue Bell family, for your continued dedication and support. The last forty-three years have been an incredible journey for all of us, but your faithfulness has strengthened you to become even stronger both personally as well as professionally.

To my church family at Central in College Station, and First Baptist Brenham, Texas. To First Baptist Broken Arrow, OK, and Alamo City, San Antonio, TX. Thank you for your continued prayers and fellowship for over forty years.

To my beautiful family, your patience, love, and encouragement mean the world. There would be no way this project would be possible without you.